OH, LIZZIE!

Elizabeth Cady Stanton in 1856, with her baby daughter Harriot
Elizabeth Cady Stanton Papers, Vassar College Library

OH, LIZZIE!
The Life of Elizabeth Cady Stanton

BY DORIS FABER

Lothrop, Lee & Shepard Company

NEW YORK

Also by Doris Faber

PETTICOAT POLITICS:
How American Women Won the Right to Vote

I WILL BE HEARD:
The Life of William Lloyd Garrison

3   4   5   75   74   73

FOR HAL

CONTENTS

•1•

THE GREEK PLOT

LITTLE YELLOW WORMS.

Drip, drip, dripping from the pale green leaves of the poplar trees along Main Street.

"E-e-e-e-e-k!" Every time Lizzie looked up and saw one, she went "E-e-e-e-e-k!" But the more she screeched, the more her sisters giggled. For they knew perfectly well that Lizzie Cady was not the least bit afraid of any old worms.

At the moment, though, as they were walking slowly home from school, Lizzie herself felt less sure about those worms than Madge and Kate did. Suppose one of the slimy things dropped onto her hair, and wriggled down a curl to touch her skin. How awful! Then a new thought struck her. No worm alive could possibly squeeze past the stiff white ruffles rubbing around her neck. She was safe! The ruffled instruments of torture her mother sewed in every dress served some purpose after all! Lizzie burst out laughing.

The Johnstown Courthouse, where Judge Cady presided
Courtesy Harper & Row
(from Mrs. Stanton's autobiography
Eighty Years and More, published in 1898)

Her sisters were not surprised. At eleven, Lizzie had already used up a large supply of their surprisability. Madge was nine and Kate eight, and as far back as they both could remember, Lizzie could always be counted on to do the unexpected.

Of course.

For doing the unexpected was not very difficult when you lived in Johnstown, New York, in the early 1800's. Most of the people there held fixed opinions on many different matters. If you happened to be a daughter of Judge Daniel Cady, your duty was clear. You were expected to behave like a proper young lady every single minute of every day.

The plain fact that no girl on earth could do this was not taken into consideration. Rules were rules in the Cady family.

As a result, even Lizzie's sisters sometimes distressed their parents. She had four sisters altogether—besides the young ones, there were two who were nearly ready to marry. Still, none of them—not Tryphena nor Harriot nor Margaret nor Catherine—ever caused Mrs. Cady to shake her head the way Elizabeth did.

Outwardly Lizzie appeared hardly different from any other well-fed girl whose father had a comfortable amount of money. True, her cheeks were pinker than was common, for she thoroughly enjoyed skating and pony riding, and her eyes were so extremely blue that they lit up her whole face. However, she had rather ordinary brown hair. Nobody ever called her beautiful.

Nor did anybody have great hopes for her. Being the middle girl in a house filled with girls was not a particularly lucky position in life, Lizzie had long since discovered. People were forever making joking remarks about how hard it would be to find a husband for her. As if that were a serious problem! As far as Lizzie herself was concerned, she would have not the slightest trouble finding a husband once she decided that was what she wanted to do. But right now, while she and Madge and Kate kept ambling homeward, there were other matters on her mind.

Why would she have to give up playing the piano this evening just because her older sisters were having visitors? Why did she have to wear the same sort of outfit Madge and Kate wore every day of the week, till they all seemed just like three peas from the same pod? Wouldn't it be more interesting to be the oldest, or even the youngest, instead of coming smack in the middle?

Yet if there was one thing Lizzie saw no sense in, that was crying over spilt milk. Anyway, she reminded herself as they walked on, if she had been able to be somebody else, she probably would have chosen to be a boy. Although boys had to fight, and handle snakes, and endure various other trials she would dislike intensely, she could not help but realize that boys also had many advantages which girls did not have. Lizzie was aware of this, for she did have one brother, Eleazur, who would be graduating from college next month.

How her father loved Eleazur! Nobody who saw the Judge greeting his only son could ever fail to notice the pride and joy on his face. Usually he gave the impression that smiling was totally out of his power, but on Eleazur he positively beamed. Lizzie had observed this even when she was still very small.

She had been born on November 12, 1815, so she had been only about three when the family suffered a terrible blow. Two other brothers died of some sickness —Lizzie had been too young at the time to be able to recall any of the details. But she never forgot what had occurred soon afterward. Moved somehow to try to console her father in his sorrow, she had climbed onto his lap to kiss him. Suddenly, almost roughly, he put her down. Eleazur had just entered the room. Forgetting that she even existed, her father reached out and clutched the boy to him. And Lizzie, weeping silently, had stood watching her brother being hugged.

Just as this scene from the past was repeating itself in her head, Lizzie and the two younger girls reached the corner of Main and Market. A wide sweep of grass stretched back from the cobbled sidewalk, and beyond this lawn a big square white house sat primly.

To the right was the ell where the Judge had his office. A separate path led toward its heavy brass-trimmed door, and Lizzie's dearest friend was polishing the shiny metal. With a most unladylike shout, she let Abraham know she was home.

How could she ever have stood that solemn house without him?

"No!"

"No, you must not do that!"

"No, you have been told that is not allowed, Elizabeth."

Polly, their nurse—and her mother—and her father —they were all forever hammering away at her as if they were sure she would slide into sin unless they held her down firmly. Only the good old Abraham seemed to understand she merely craved some harmless amusement. Whenever the chorus of "No! No! No!" started, he would roll his eyes at her in sympathy. If she was sent upstairs without dessert, he would smuggle her a piece of pie. His heart was as loving as his skin was black, and Lizzie felt warmer to him than to anybody else in the whole world.

That was why she rushed to find Abraham a few weeks later when the dreadful news arrived about her brother, Eleazur.

There had been an accident. Two carriages had collided. Eleazur had been killed!

Tears streaming from her eyes, Lizzie sought out Abraham down in the cellar where he was repairing some old barrels. It took several minutes till she could get calm enough to tell him what had happened. Then he held her close, while his soothing voice kept trying to make her feel better. At last she began to hear the words he was saying, and two of them shook her out of her own grief.

Her father!

What fierce pain *he* must be feeling this very minute!

The dim light of the cellar seemed to change, and once more Lizzie was seeing her father clutch at her brother long ago. But now her memory was somewhat different. Instead of the hurt she had felt at being pushed aside, she was happy for her father's sake because he still had one child he deeply loved.

But suppose that could be true again!

What if she changed herself? Couldn't she do something so special that her father would be as fond of her as he had been of Eleazur?

Since Lizzie could never have an idea without immediately trying to act on it, she began right that instant to work out some plans. However, she quickly saw that even if she were polite and obedient and cheerful all the time, she would still fail. It was not for his good manners that Eleazur had been so highly valued. It was mainly, Lizzie realized, just because he was a boy.

Yet why did her father value boys so much more than girls?

Wasn't there anything a girl could do to make her father feel proud of her?

All the rest of that miserable day, Lizzie twisted and turned those questions in her mind. Finally, after she had finished saying her prayers, she found the answers she wanted. Before she fell asleep that night, she had hatched out a plot.

Early the next morning Lizzie slipped from her bed while Kate and Madge were still asleep. She dressed swiftly, then stole down the stairs and out the back door into the cool, dewy yard. Not a soul saw her as she scurried toward the row of bushes that marked the end of the Cady property.

Holding her skirt above her ankles, she started running. Then she slowed to a more sedate pace on reaching the narrow path through the hedge. Hooray! Dr. Hosack was out working in his vegetable garden already.

"Good morning, sir," she called to him.

Dr. Hosack was the pastor of their church, and on Sundays when he stood up in the pulpit his rumbling sermons fearfully bored her. Yet Lizzie had found out

a long time ago that on weekdays, and especially when
he was hoeing his vegetables, he was a very nice man.
She trusted him completely, and came right to the
point.

"Doctor, which do you like best, boys or girls?" she
demanded.

Behind his spectacles, the pastor's eyes twinkled.
"Why girls, to be sure," he said. "I would not give you
for all the boys in the world."

But Lizzie was in no mood for teasing. In her most
serious voice, she blurted out:

"My father prefers boys, and I intend to be as near
like one as possible. So I have decided to give up playing. I wish to prove I can be as clever and as brave as
any boy. I'm going to practice jumping over fences on
horseback, and I want to learn Greek. Will you give
me a Greek lesson now?"

Dr. Hosack gravely put down his hoe. "Yes, child,"
he said. "Come into my library, and we will begin
without delay."

If Lizzie had thought that learning another language
would be as easy as falling off a log, she quickly grasped
this was not the case. Her first glance at the shabby
book Dr. Hosack took down from a shelf showed her
she had a real chore ahead of her. Even the letters of
the Greek alphabet were entirely different from English
letters. How could she make the slightest sense out of
those strange scratchings?

But when Lizzie made up her mind to do something,
she did not like to admit defeat. Every spare minute

from that morning onward, she sat up in her room with Dr. Hosack's book, going over and over the first few pages. Several times a week she hurried through the back hedge to ask him more questions. After school ended, she was tempted to put aside her plans till the end of the summer, or at least to concentrate on her other idea of training herself as a daredevil rider, but she could guess that if she once quit the Greek it would be much harder to start again.

So she doggedly kept at the lessons Dr. Hosack gave her, and soon she was able to feel a small thrill of achievement. She could actually read the first exercises in the Greek grammar book! From the way her teacher smiled at her, she felt sure she was beginning to make some progress.

Yet Lizzie had no idea of how much she was amazing Dr. Hosack. Naturally he knew about her brother's tragic death, and he had been touched by Lizzie's unusual scheme for comforting her father. Each time she appeared for another lesson, though, he became more convinced that he ought to have a talk with Judge Cady. So one afternoon the pastor called on him and they conferred privately for several hours.

The next morning Lizzie was summoned to her father's office. Since his children were not supposed to disturb him there, she had hardly ever entered this mysterious chamber. In contrast with the bright sunshine outside, its dark walls looked so forbidding that Lizzie felt almost frightened.

But as her eyes adjusted to the gloom, she saw that

her father was not frowning. On her every past visit,
even when she had done nothing to displease him, he
had appeared to be as gloomy as the furnishings, and
although she could not imagine why he had sent for
her on this occasion, she was startled. Not only was her
father not frowning, he actually seemed to have a
shadow of a smile around his lips!

"Sit down, my daughter," he said, and now there
could be no mistake. He *was* smiling at her. "I have
had an interesting conversation with Dr. Hosack," he
went on.

Lizzie's heart beat fast. Her father knew about her
Greek plot! And he was not angry!

Indeed, he was pleased, he told her, so pleased that
he was accepting a suggestion Dr. Hosack had been
kind enough to offer. In the school she attended with
her sisters, he knew she was learning only simple subjects. While he did not approve of burdening girls with
information that they could have no possible use for
in their future lives—suddenly Lizzie felt an impulse to
protest, but stifled it—still, he was impressed to hear
that his daughter had a remarkably keen mind. Therefore he was changing his plans for her.

He understood that there were a few girls enrolled
in the Johnstown Academy where boys from well-off
families in the area were prepared for attending college. Since girls of course could never dream of attending college—again Lizzie was tempted to interrupt but
did not—the subjects they could study at the academy

were limited. Nevertheless, he had just spoken with the headmaster.

So Judge Cady's daughter Elizabeth would be welcomed at the Academy starting in September, and she would even be allowed to study Greek.

Then, having said all this, the Judge showed how his feelings toward her were still torn between pride and disappointment.

"Oh, my daughter," the Judge added, "would that you had been a boy!"

As her father spoke these words and then sighed deeply, tears filled Lizzie's eyes. Yet they were tears of joy as well as sadness. For already her plot had begun to work. In another month, she would be the only girl in a class of boys learning Greek, and what an opportunity that would be!

Then she would have a real chance to prove how intelligent a girl could be. She remembered that when Eleazur had been at the Johnstown Academy, a prize had been awarded at the end of the year to the student with the highest marks in Greek. Unfortunately, her brother had just missed winning. Even though she was a girl, she was determined to bring that prize home to Judge Cady!

From her first day at the Academy that was Lizzie's goal, and she stuck to it. With its dingy brick walls and strict teachers, the new school often depressed her. No matter that she had longed to be on her own, she missed having Madge and Kate always trailing after her. Yet she never forgot her aim of taking first prize in Greek.

Being Lizzie, she could not be serious all the time. After some of the boys in her class took to untying her hair ribbons whenever the teacher's back was turned, she thought of a trick to distract their attention. She started a contest to see who could draw the most comical picture of Mr. Parker.

In her other classes, she became good friends with several girls. They were all older than she was, and they gave her some new ideas.

One of her new friends was the daughter of the sheriff, and as a result Lizzie got in the habit of sneaking into the jail on the way home from school. At first, the reason was simply that she wanted to see what desperadoes looked like, but after finding that the inhabitants of Johnstown's lockup were mainly poor fellows with the failing of drinking too much whisky, she began trying to reform them by taking them cake and candy.

Another of the girls she met at the Academy was the daughter of the local hotelkeeper. This friendship led to her helping out on busy Saturdays by serving in the dining room, but Lizzie was far more interested in eavesdropping than in being a waitress. Once when she heard two lawyers talking about a case that sounded exciting, she stopped in her tracks to listen.

"Child, you'd better attend to business," one of the men warned her. "Bring me a glass of water."

"I am not a servant," Lizzie told him indignantly. "I am here for fun."

Still, her foremost goal all during that year was to excel in school, and she succeeded. On the last day, when the prizes were awarded, the top honors in Greek went to Miss Elizabeth Cady.

She rushed homeward, carrying her prize triumphantly. It was a handsome Greek book, with her name written on the cover in gold letters. Heedless of the fact that her father was not supposed to be disturbed while he was in his office, she ran directly to his big door and pulled it open.

Seated at his desk, Judge Cady looked up in surprise as she entered.

"There!" Lizzie said, and she put the book down in front of him. "I won it."

Her father rose from his chair and held out his arms to her. But the expression on his long, thin face combined pride and love with another sort of feeling. He leaned over and kissed Lizzie on the forehead. "Ah!" he sighed. "You should have been a boy!"

·2·

ANOTHER PRIZE

EVEN THOUGH WINNING HER GREEK AWARD DID NOT accomplish all that Lizzie had hoped, it made quite a difference. From then on, there was an unspoken understanding between her and her father. Of his five daughters, the middle one clearly pleased him the most.

Not that Lizzie suddenly turned into a model of polite good manners, as Judge Cady would have wished. On the contrary, she still exploded every so often in the unlikeliest way. Shortly after the end of the school term a special treat was approved, at least partly to reward her for earning her prize—and she blew up almost as spectacularly as a whole bushel of fireworks.

The treat was a trip to visit Grandmother Cady seventy miles away, on the far side of Albany. Doubtless the main reason for the journey was to provide a change of scene for Lizzie's mother, who had been in low spirits ever since the loss of Eleazur. Mrs. Cady was a tall and queenly woman who always went about her duties as if her thoughts were really absorbed on some other matter, but since her son's death her mind had seemed even more removed than usual. Her husband must have thought it might distract her, and also offer Elizabeth some new opportunities, if he sent them off together. He was absolutely right.

But since Elizabeth would be missed by her younger sisters, the Judge decided that Margaret and Catherine might as well go too. That was his mistake.

Had Lizzie set out with only her mother, she probably would have behaved in a rather restrained fashion. As it was, though, the party required two carriages. Nurse Polly accompanied Mrs. Cady in the more comfortable one, while the three girls, with Abraham cracking the whip, followed in less elegant style.

So Lizzie felt no need to hold back her enthusiasm. This was her first trip out of their own county, and seeing new sights excited her enormously. Once they left the familiar cobbled streets of Johnstown, their road followed the winding Mohawk River eastward. At every twist and bend, Lizzie gave a fresh cry of delight at the little bridge or ferry boat she spied, or at some other picturesque feature of the green, hilly farmland through which they were passing.

Yet she did have to sit comparatively still, and a huge charge of energy built up inside her. When they stopped for lunch, it broke loose.

They had reached the small city of Schenectady.

This appeared to be only a somewhat larger version of Johnstown till they entered the splendid dining room of the hotel there. Then Lizzie was suddenly struck by a gorgeous painting on the wall, and she forgot that she was to take her seat quietly at the table where her mother was already waiting.

Instead she grabbed Madge's arm. "Oh, look!" Lizzie said. "It's Noah and his Ark." And she dashed over to see the picture at closer range, narrowly missing a waiter carrying a tray of water glasses. No matter! Just beyond the picture of Noah, she saw another painting in even brighter colors. "It's Moses in the bulrushes!" she shouted. Why, on every wall there were paintings of her favorite scenes from the Bible!

By now, both of her younger sisters had caught Lizzie's excitement. All three of the Cady girls rushed from painting to painting, screaming to each other as they recognized the subject being depicted. None of them had the slightest notion that practically every other guest in the dining room was laughing uproariously at their performance.

Their mother, though, was more embarrassed than she had ever been in her life. As soon as her girls could be calmed down, she let them know how they had disgraced her. Then she banished them to eat in a separate room as if they were still little children.

Even Abraham, leading them to this makeshift nursery, shook his head at Lizzie. "Now you ought not to act as if you had just come out of the woods and never saw anything before," he said severely.

So for the rest of the trip Lizzie did try her best to behave more properly. At the hotel in Albany where they stayed overnight, she held herself back from racing outside when she heard a band playing in the street, and merely almost fell out of a window in her eagerness to watch the show. At Grandmother Cady's farm she submitted meekly to being kissed by countless aunts and uncles, and only occasionally in the course of their visit stirred up enough commotion for her mother to write home about. As a result, the lecture she received from her father when she returned to Johnstown was not too sharp.

In fact, he let it be known in a number of indirect ways as the months passed that he did not mind having her spend a free hour now and then keeping him company in his office. Lizzie came to look forward to pulling open the heavy door and taking a cool glass of cider in to him or even a bowl of flowers to brighten the room. Usually they would exchange only a few words before he went back to working over some papers on his desk. Then she would curl up in a chair with one of his law books.

At first Lizzie found these dreadfully dull, but then her father explained that laws were not meant to be entertaining, and that they contained more truth than any novel by Sir Walter Scott. For the law books held all the rules civilized people had agreed on as the best way of settling any problem that arose. Because his voice had such conviction when he talked about the importance of the books in his library, Lizzie tried sampling pages at random, to see if she could share his feelings on this subject.

The law must be something like Greek, she told herself. If once you picked up the general idea, then you could figure out the most complicated sentences. So she kept hoping to find some basic clues in her father's books, but she took care not to let him guess what she gradually concluded.

She would like to become a lawyer!

It would not do, though, to tell Judge Cady that. In his mind, she could plainly gather, a female could not possibly aim for such an important position. Even a girl capable of learning Greek was not clever enough to master the mysteries of the law. Well, that was his opinion, Lizzie said to herself. In time she would show him, but meanwhile she merely sat quietly and cozily, and to all appearances aimlessly, turning the pages of his books.

While she did so, occasionally a visitor came to consult her father. If the caller happened to be a woman, Lizzie paid particular attention to the conversation. Maybe she might hear something that would help her in her plan for becoming a lawyer. That was what she thought at first, but she soon learned otherwise.

Not only were there no female lawyers, the law itself was horribly unfair to all women!

Sitting unnoticed in her father's office, Lizzie nearly burst while she listened to one conversation after another that made these two conclusions unmistakable.

The last straw was a tearful appeal to Judge Cady by a sweet old Scottish lady who in her younger days had helped out with their family's laundry.

It seemed that she had inherited a good sum of money from a relative in Scotland. But her husband had spent much of this on one foolish scheme or another before dying a poor man. Now her only son, a scoundrel if ever there was one, was threatening to turn her out into the cold without a penny. So would the Judge please help her keep her own cottage and her own small fortune? Would he show her how the law could help her?

While Mrs. MacPherson was speaking, Judge Cady kept slowly shaking his head. When she finished, he rubbed hard at his chin. Then he told her the sad truth. Alas, the law could not help her. The law said that a married woman could not own any property. Even the money her own family had given to her belonged by law to her husband, and after the death of her husband the law gave her son the right to do whatever he chose with it. As far as the law was concerned, she had no rights at all.

Lizzie could hardly hold in her sputtering. What sort of nonsense was this? Was a nice old woman like Mrs. MacPherson expected to starve if her son was mean enough to put her out of her own cottage? Any law that let such a cruel thing happen did not deserve to stay in the book.

By this time, Lizzie was past fourteen but she was

still unpredictable. Her father sighed as she jumped up right after Mrs. MacPherson left and then hurried outside. He would have done more than sigh if he had known what his daughter was planning now.

On the path leading toward the street, Lizzie caught up with the old lady. "Please, Mrs. MacPherson, you must not worry any further," she told her earnestly. "I've thought of how to help you."

"Ah, you're a good girl, Lizzie," Mrs. MacPherson said. "But there's nothing can be done, your father made that obvious."

"Oh, yes, there is!" Lizzie insisted. "Any law that lets your son treat you so badly is a bad law. The books have some others, too, that are unfair to women, and I have been marking a little check mark beside them. As soon as I find yours, I'll mark it in the same way. Then I'll cut them all out some night after my father has gone to sleep."

Mrs. MacPherson stared at Lizzie doubtfully. "I do not want you to get in any trouble, my dear," she said. Then her own trouble overcame her again, and she resumed slowly walking toward the street.

But several hours later, Mrs. MacPherson had second thoughts and she took up her shawl to walk over to Main Street once more. So it happened that Judge Cady had an unexpected visitor while Lizzie was upstairs doing schoolwork after supper.

His face was a study in mixed feelings when he saw Mrs. MacPherson to the door after hearing what she had to say, and also pressing into her hand a substantial sum of his own money. He had intended ever since that afternoon to see that she was taken care of somehow, yet his daughter had certainly forced him to act more swiftly and directly than he would have done without her interference.

Oh, Lizzie! He nearly said the words aloud. For this daughter would be the death of him. *What* would she not think of next? But then the Judge reflected that at least part of the trouble stemmed from her not knowing things she had no way of knowing. Perhaps she needed more of an education than even the Johnstown Academy was providing?

Needless to say, there could be no question of college because no colleges existed that would accept a female student. And rightly so, the Judge sincerely believed. Since the only acceptable future for a girl was to become a wife and mother, why confuse her with knowledge she could never use?

Yet Elizabeth might not find a husband who suited her, her father realized. In that case, should any misfortune overtake him, she might even have to earn her own keep someday. Since the only respectable occupation for a gently brought up young lady was teaching, here was another reason to consider giving her the best possible schooling. Right then and there, the Judge resolved to inquire about the seminary for girls that Mrs. Emma Willard had recently established in the nearby city of Troy.

Knowing nothing of her father's second conversation with Mrs. MacPherson, or of the many questions this had raised in his mind, Lizzie was startled a few days later when he put aside his papers as she entered his office. "I wish to speak to you, Elizabeth," he said in a more serious tone than he had lately used with her. What had she done to make him so solemn?

Then as soon as he spoke a few more sentences, Lizzie understood. He made no reference to Mrs. MacPherson, and she thought he was being careful not to hurt her feelings, but his meaning could not be missed when he explained to her that there were lawyers and law libraries all over the State of New York. So if any laws were to be removed from his own books, there would still be no difference in women's legal condition.

"When you are grown up and able to prepare a speech," he said, "you might go down to Albany and talk to the lawmakers there. Tell them all you have seen in this office—the sufferings of poor women deprived of their legal rights—and if you can persuade these men to pass new laws, the old ones will be dead letters."

Lizzie nodded. Of course what he was saying made sense, now that she considered it. But her father had not finished.

In a surprisingly warmer tone, he went on to tell her he had come to appreciate the fact that she was a rather unusual young lady. He did not say he had slight when the girls were taken on their daily walk through Troy's streets.

Best of all, she made good friends with several of the other students. One thing about them amazed her, though. They were so unused to being around boys that the mere sight of young men walking past the school building caused great excitement. Once while she was sitting quietly reading a girl near the window called, "Heads out!" Lizzie ran with all the rest.

"What is it?" she asked, expecting to be told that a giraffe or some other wonder fit for a museum was passing below.

"Why, don't you see those boys?" another girl demanded.

"Oh," said Lizzie, "is that all? I have seen boys all my life."

Yet she had to admit that being in a school with only girls made the appearance of any boy more interesting. There was a rule that no boy could call on a girl or even write to her unless he was her brother or cousin. As a result, many of the girls turned up with an astonishing number of relatives, and the amount of time they all spent talking about boys far exceeded the amount spent on any other subject. If boys and girls attended the same school, there would be no cause for such a strange state of affairs to develop, Lizzie decided. That was one more reason she disapproved of Mrs. Willard's establishment.

As for that lady in person, not till after Lizzie came

hope that she would willingly follow the example of her older sisters, both of whom were now engaged to marry promising law students he fully approved of as acceptable sons-in-law.

What the Judge did say was that he had decided Elizabeth should have a taste of higher education. So he had arranged for her to enter Mrs. Willard's new school for girls over in Troy.

Lizzie jumped up and threw her arms around him. Here was a plan she liked! This meant she would not have to envy the boys in her class who were going on to college. Why, it was almost as if she had just won another prize!

Lizzie's high hopes lasted through the next several months. When autumn rolled around again and it was time for her to depart, her spirits were further raised by her finding out that a grand new adventure was also in store for her. After going with her mother from Johnstown to Schenectady by coach, they were to ride on one of the first railroad lines in the whole United States.

Upon boarding a train of the new cars in Schenectady, she was astounded to note the method that had been adopted for pulling the passengers up a steep hill at the city's outskirts. Another car at the top of the hill was filled with heavy stones, then allowed to descend the opposite side, thereby dragging her own conveyance up toward the summit. During the rest of the journey a steam locomotive proved equal to the task of tugging them along, but it did seem to Lizzie that a more sensible way of coping with that hill could have been found. Why not put the tracks in a tunnel under the hill, or better still just go around it?

Yet Lizzie quite forgot the excitement of having sampled a new mode of travel right after she arrived in Troy. Her spirits dropped then. Indeed they dropped lower than she could ever remember.

Not only did she feel terribly lonely the minute her mother left her. That she could have borne if this prize had been the least bit what she had expected. But from the instant she set foot in the ladylike parlor where new girls were welcomed, Lizzie could tell that she did not really belong here.

Manners, manners, manners! All day long, the girls at Mrs. Willard's were gently urged to mind their manners. "Speak more slowly, Elizabeth, please do." "There is no excuse for leaning across the dining table." "A young lady must always stand perfectly straight." It was not for constant comments like these that Lizzie had come away from her own home.

Even more disappointing, though, the course of study she had hoped to find did not exist at Mrs. Willard's school. Already she had a good grounding in Greek, Latin and mathematics, and she had been planning to go on with these subjects. She also wanted to learn enough in other areas to be able somehow to follow through on her dream of becoming a lawyer. It was to pursue a serious program for improving her mind that she had come to Troy.

But instead of solid geometry, she found herself in a class discussing a vague topic described as "intellectual philosophy." Instead of going more deeply into Latin and Greek, she was given "moral philosophy." Music lessons were offered as a substitute for science.

However, in the case of one branch of science Mrs. Willard had the advanced idea that girls deserved instruction. This was physiology, which concerned itself with the workings of the human body. Because women were so often given the responsibility for treating sickness in their own families, Mrs. Willard thought every girl should not only learn basic health rules but also should understand why these were advisable. At a time when respectable women were supposed to be protected from any unpleasant fact of life, teaching girls about the reasons for upset stomachs was considered very daring—except by Lizzie Cady. If she ever felt particularly glum during her first weeks in Troy, Lizzie liked to imagine her own mother entering one of the class rooms and discovering that the drawing on th blackboard represented the human digestive syste Picturing the shocked look on Mrs. Cady's face ne failed to make Lizzie laugh.

But as week after week went by, Lizzie found o reasons to feel more cheerful. She did love musi she relished her chance to take guitar lessons. Th the food served in the dining hall was miserab was comforted by discovering where to buy d little cakes right around the corner from the She managed to dart in frequently to make a

Mrs. Emma Willard's seminary in Troy, 1830
Courtesy Harper & Row
(from Mrs. Stanton's autobiography *Eighty Years and More,*
published in 1898)

back from Johnstown to start her second year in Troy
did she lay eyes on the school's famous founder. Widely
known as a pioneer in the cause of female education,
Mrs. Willard had spent the preceding twelve months
traveling around Europe spreading word of her unusual venture.

There was no doubt that Mrs. Willard was an im-
pressive-looking woman, Lizzie had to agree. Robed
always in black silk or satin, she had an air of authority
that struck awe in the beholder. Lizzie was also willing
to admit that at least some of her ideas made good
sense. For example, her policy of giving scholarships to
several girls from poor families, so they would be able

to earn a decent living as teachers, was a very worthy effort.

But, as Lizzie tried unsuccessfully to tell her father, this school fell short—oh, so sadly short—of filling her own needs. Why could she not go to a real college? What if no other girl had yet been admitted to any college in the area? At the Johnstown Academy she had proved she could earn the highest marks, competing equally with boys. She would not even mind being the only girl in a classroom—indeed, she would rather like the challenge.

Still, none of her arguments had moved her father, and so here she was again.

Lizzie truly did try to forget her disappointment as that year progressed. She poured much of her stifled mental energy into writing English compositions, a chore she thoroughly enjoyed. Nevertheless, she could not help feeling hopelessly bored most of the time.

In this unsettled state of mind, she went with the other girls in the school that spring to hear a noted preacher who had just come to conduct a series of prayer meetings in Troy. He was the Reverend Charles G. Finney, a fiery speaker. During the past several years he had made a great name for himself by arousing audiences all over the country.

Lizzie had never given much thought to religion before listening to the Reverend Finney. But suddenly his voice caught her rapt attention. He was telling about hell and the devil, and about the long procession of sinners being swept downward, soon to make the awful plunge into the burning depths of liquid fire below. Then all at once he paused, and silently pointed a finger at the supposed procession.

"There!" he shouted. "Do you not see them?"

Lizzie almost fell from her seat, so terrifying was the vision before her eyes. Not only did she clearly see the mass of sinners he was describing, but right among their number she also saw herself.

Night after night, Lizzie feared to close her eyes because that awful scene would flash into her mind again. If she finally fell asleep, she awoke in a cold sweat of horror. Her dread became so real to her that she lost interest in all else.

When her parents came to fetch her at the end of the term, they seemed startled by her appearance. Lizzie could not bear to speak about the reason for her distress, but under close questioning by the Judge she finally confessed. He said no more then. Only after they had almost reached home did he turn to his wife and make an announcement:

"Mrs. Cady, I believe this entire family will profit from a complete change during the next several weeks. Therefore, will you please prepare for a journey to inspect the Niagara Falls."

A HAPPY MISTAKE

AFTER RETURNING FROM THAT GLORIOUS TRIP TO NI-
agara, Lizzie felt her spirits so elevated by the wonders
she had seen that she slipped contentedly into a pleasant new routine. Now she had finished with Mrs.
Willard, and she was nearly seventeen. She had reached
a delightful turning point.

Everybody agreed that she was no longer a child.
She was allowed to choose her own clothing and to
arrange her hair to suit herself. Polly and her parents
let her do as she wished much of the time. In short,
she was treated almost like a grown person.

Lizzie was shrewd enough to note that her new freedom had its limits. Should she take it into her head
to wear purple spangles in the style of a circus per-
former, or to sit up in a tree shouting poetry at the
top of her voice, she would certainly be stopped. Her
conduct was still supposed to remain within definite
bounds, and her first goal in life was still supposed to

be the same. Above all else, she was expected to attract a good husband, as her own mother had done at the age of sixteen.

Toward this end, even the sharp-faced Polly now encouraged Lizzie to sing and dance. Whenever a group of young people came calling, Abraham was summoned to bring out his fiddle and to scratch away tune after tune by the fireside while the room shook with the pounding of dancing feet. Fresh doughnuts and jugs of sweet cider appeared as if by magic.

Naturally, Lizzie enjoyed all this. Hay rides and sleigh rides—the whole assortment of pleasures deemed suitable for courting couples provided great fun, she thought. Yet she also loved to play chess, and she could see no reason why she should not play to win.

That was her trouble, other people in her family kept suggesting. Her oldest sister, Tryphena, already married but still living at home while her husband studied law with Judge Cady, tried hard to enlighten Lizzie. "Men don't feel comfortable with a girl who seems too clever," she explained. "Lizzie, you must let them beat you if you don't wish to frighten them away."

However, Lizzie refused to take such comments to heart. Any young man who could be frightened away so easily did not deserve her, she would say in an airy tone. What she did not say was that she had increasingly grave doubts about whether she would ever want to get married.

As month after month passed, she saw fewer and

fewer reasons for making any change. Why should she give up this marvelous freedom? For if she did marry, that was precisely what she would be doing. She would be exchanging her new freedom for a condition hardly better than slavery.

Oh, yes! Marriage was a form of slavery, Lizzie decided all by herself. Knowing well how strongly her parents would oppose this opinion, she did not speak of it—except to her brother-in-law and some of his fellow law students. Indeed, it was they who made her see the real evils of the married state.

With her ambition to become a lawyer still buried deeply in her mind, Lizzie was drawn to her father's office whenever she felt at loose ends. There she often found her brother-in-law, Edward Bayard, the son of Senator Bayard from Delaware and a college classmate of Eleazur's. Edward and the other young men who kept turning up to study with Judge Cady took pleasure in teasing Lizzie.

Once they had discovered her special interest in laws affecting women, they made a game of searching out the worst laws they could find. Some were so comical Lizzie could not help laughing, but others nearly made her cry. Whether funny or sad, their message was the same—if a woman married, she herself and all her property legally belonged to her husband.

Edward made this ridiculously clear when she came into the office on the morning of her eighteenth birthday to show him the coral necklace she had just received from her parents. After admiring the beads, he smiled broadly at Lizzie and said, "If somehow it should happen that you became my wife, then these would be mine. I could take them and lock them up, and you could never wear them except with my permission. I could even exchange them for a cigar, and you could watch them evaporate in smoke."

While Lizzie understood that Edward was only teasing her, she took him seriously in one respect. To herself, she vowed then that she would never marry.

Once having come to this private decision, Lizzie still enjoyed her life most of the time. Excused from any household chores except ironing her own clothing, she was free to read, ride, or play music whenever she wished. Excellent meals appeared on the table thrice daily, without any effort on her part. And to vary the monotony of staying close to home, she could take interesting trips whenever she chose. After Edward started to practice law in New York City, she could visit him and Tryphena several weeks every year. Or she could stay with her sister Harriot who had moved there, too, after marrying. In addition, friends from school kept inviting her to their homes, and so did numerous cousins and aunts.

So the years passed busily, if rather aimlessly, till Lizzie was nearing her twenty-fourth birthday. Then it happened that she was asked to spend a month with her cousin, Lib Smith, over in Peterboro in the central part of the state. Since the month in question was

Lizzie Cady as a young woman

August, Lizzie looked forward to leaving the dust and heat of Johnstown for the cooler countryside. She also looked forward to meeting an unusual group of people, because Lib's parents were known for the broad range of their hospitality. At their home, you were likely to find every variety of guest, from members of Congress to runaway slaves being sheltered on their way to Canada. It was in Peterboro that Elizabeth Cady met Henry B. Stanton.

He was a tall man with a large mustache, and he was ten years older than Lizzie. At first glance, she could see that most people would consider him handsome, but that could hardly matter to her, she assured herself. Not only was she still set on remaining single, but also it appeared that Mr. Stanton had already made other plans. For he arrived at the Smith mansion with a blond young woman, and Lizzie naturally assumed they were engaged.

Nevertheless, she found herself deeply interested in Mr. Stanton—if not in his person, at least in his profession. He was a reformer, Cousin Lib's father had explained. Being of the same tribe himself, Gerrit Smith had a large number of friends whose main goal in life was to reform or improve the world one way or another. Henry Stanton's principal aim was to end slavery in the United States, and he had become one of the leading figures in the antislavery movement. In fact, he was stopping in Peterboro so that he could speak at a series of meetings arranged by local abolitionists, as the people working to abolish slavery were coming to be called.

It was Mr. Stanton's cause that really appealed to her, Lizzie told herself. She had been feeling restless lately, and perhaps her mind was craving some new activity. Then why not attend these abolitionist meetings?

So every morning for the next several weeks, she joined the carriage load of guests departing from the

Smith house with Henry Stanton. Each day, it seemed that their route took them past even more beautiful hills and valleys than they had noted on the previous day. But besides the lovely countryside they saw in all directions, these rides also offered lively talk on countless topics. Being sure that Mr. Stanton could have no possible reason for paying any special attention to her, Lizzie spoke up without the slightest shyness with him. She chattered and laughed as freely as if he were merely one of her brothers-in-law.

She found herself coming to admire him greatly as she listened to him speak at meeting after meeting. Ever since she had fallen under the spell of the Reverend Finney while in Troy, Lizzie had known that she had a weakness for the thunder-and-lightning type of speechmaker. Let anyone pound away at her from up on a platform, and she could hardly help feeling convinced. Yet she really did not believe Mr. Stanton was merely a spellbinder.

No, he seemed far too intelligent. True, he knew all the tricks of the orator's trade. He could make an audience laugh, and he could make them weep. But beyond her realizing that Henry Stanton could probably stir her emotions by merely reading a dictionary aloud, Lizzie also admired his position on the issue of slavery. Here was a man—and a cause—she could sincerely respect.

Thus as the weeks sped by, Lizzie found herself wishing time would pass more slowly. Soon Mr. Stanton's series of meetings would end, and soon she would have to return to Johnstown. How dull life would seem then!

But toward the end of her stay, there came a morning when no meeting was scheduled. After breakfast, Mr. Stanton joined Lizzie on the porch where she was walking up and down enjoying the balmy air. "Since we have no other plans for the day, what do you say to a ride on horseback?" he asked.

Lizzie agreed instantly, then went to change her clothing. While doing so, an odd thought struck her. Suppose the blond young woman who had arrived with Mr. Stanton, and then departed shortly afterward, did not really intend to marry him? No, that was most unlikely, for any young woman who won this man's heart could scarcely be expected to turn him down. Could she do it herself? Almost angrily, Lizzie pushed the question out of her mind, not allowing herself to stop and wonder why her old vow to avoid becoming no better than a slave to any man no longer seemed terribly important.

Yet she was not quite as astonished as she tried to pretend when Mr. Stanton urged her to stop her horse while they were passing a particularly fine grove of trees. Dismounting, he walked over and laid his hand on her saddle. "Shall we walk a bit here?" he suggested.

Then as they strolled alone among those trees, he spoke the words she had wished he would say to her, even though she had not let herself admit it. And she gave him the reply he wanted to hear, because now she realized that she had come to love him. When they resumed their ride, Lizzie was engaged to marry Henry Stanton.

But what about the blond young woman?

Oh, she was merely the daughter of an old friend of his family.

Thank goodness, Lizzie said to herself, and she meant it in two ways. For had she not believed that Henry was already taken, she would certainly have done her best to keep her vow and avoid captivating him. So she would always be grateful to this other woman for being the unwitting cause of such a happy mistake.

Still another matter troubled Lizzie, though. While she could see now that she really wanted to spend the rest of her life with her dear Henry, would she be able to become a good wife? How could she possibly agree to give up all her own rights, and to be ruled by any man?

On that score she need have no worries, Henry assured her. For he believed just as she did that women deserved better treatment. In his eyes, marriage should be a partnership, with two equal partners, and he was perfectly willing to make every possible effort toward that end.

However, if Lizzie thought no other problem remained, she quickly found out that she was wrong. As soon as Cousin Lib's father heard their news, he tried to warn her of trouble ahead. Knowing Judge Cady, he knew just what the Judge's reaction would be.

"Out of the question!"

Lizzie's father meant it, too. No matter if Henry
Stanton came of an old Connecticut family, and that
the B. in his name stood for a Brewster who had sailed
on the *Mayflower*. No matter that Mr. Stanton had
the good judgment to admire his daughter. Mr. Stanton had no fit position in life, and he could not expect
Miss Cady to become his wife.

It was bad enough that Cousin Gerrit Smith amused
himself with all this abolition foolishness, Judge Cady
fumed. Much worse, though, here was a young man
lacking any regular source of income, such as Gerrit
Smith had inherited, and still he spent all his time aid-
ing wild-eyed reformers bent on causing trouble between the North and the South. Let people in the
Southern states take care of their own affairs, the Judge
said firmly. And let this Mr. Stanton find some honest
business of *his* own before he dared to see Elizabeth
again.

Lizzie tried to explain to her father that Henry had
earned his living for almost twenty years by writing
for newspapers as well as by giving lectures on other
topics besides slavery. Yet the Judge refused to heed
her.

The man was a dangerous radical, he told her. And
impractical. Not at all an acceptable son-in-law.

What could Lizzie do? Week after week for that
whole winter, she tried to decide what her course
should be. It pained her so much to think of marrying

against her family's wishes that she finally wrote to
Henry and told him that she wanted to break their
engagement. Maybe her original plan of not marrying
was the most sensible.

But Henry wrote back and proposed a different plan.

He told her that within the next few months he
would be going on a voyage to England, to attend a
meeting there of antislavery forces from all over the
world. As a means of paying his expenses, he had arranged to write articles about conditions abroad for
two leading newspapers in New York City and Washington. Gathering material overseas would take him
the better part of a year, and he could not calmly endure the prospect of being separated from her that long.

Therefore, would she not sail with him?

The trip could be their honeymoon, he wrote. If she
would but agree to marry him, he would arrange
everything.

To run away, to elope! The bold scheme thrilled
Lizzie, besides terrifying her, but she agreed to it.

How she managed to survive the next few weeks she
could never say. Somehow her parents did not suspect
her secret. As her excuse for packing several boxes and
a trunk, she said she was going to visit the Bayards
down in New York City, and indeed she was, though
only for a few days. After that . . .

No, Lizzie could scarcely let herself think any further.

By now all of her sisters were married, and she did
tell her plans to them. For if her parents could not be

present at her wedding, she still wanted the rest of her family with her on this momentous occasion.

So it happened that a small group of relatives was on hand when Miss Elizabeth Cady stood up facing a minister she had never seen before, on May 10, 1840. She was wearing a simple white gown that was the best her sister Tryphena could provide without having had the bride available for painstaking fittings by a seamstress. Lizzie's brother-in-law Edward held her arm, prepared to do the office of giving her away to her prospective husband.

Suddenly a question occurred to Lizzie. Exactly what did this minister intend to say in the marriage ceremony? The gentleman seemed rather surprised by the question, but he rapidly told her the words he would use.

"No!" Lizzie shook her head decisively. "You must leave out the word, 'obey.' I absolutely refuse to obey someone with whom I am entering into an equal relationship."

Henry Stanton looked startled, as if he had just discovered what might be in store for him. Nevertheless, he nodded to the minister.

And so the word "obey" was not included in the ceremony that started then. When it ended a few minutes later, Lizzie Cady signed the register for the first time with her new name. Elizabeth Cady Stanton.

°4°

TO LONDON~~

THEIR VOYAGE ACROSS THE OCEAN COULD HARDLY HAVE
been more delightful to the new Mrs. Stanton. Going
on a trip had always made her particularly cheerful,
and this trip had the added novelty of being her first
experience as a married woman. There were definite
advantages that came of having an attentive husband
looking after her comfort at every opportunity, she
noticed right away. Her only regret was that she had
not met and married Henry sooner.

It even amused her when an acquaintance of Henry's,
who was also traveling to the antislavery conference in
London, seemed pained by her lively manner. This
Mr. Birney was a gentleman of the old school, rather
like her own father. Teasingly, she urged him to tell
her whenever she did something he could not approve
of, so that she could correct her ways. He immediately
took her at her word.

"Several times I have heard you call your husband
'Henry' in the presence of strangers, which is not per-

missible in polite society," Mr. Birney informed her. "You should always say, 'Mr. Stanton.' " For this advice she gravely thanked him, and she did try from then on to behave more stiffly when she was among strangers.

In this effort, she was aided by the fact that she had given herself a task to accomplish on shipboard. Knowing so little about the antislavery movement, she decided to read all she could about it, in order to be able to follow the discussions in London more intelligently. Therefore she spent many hours of their nineteen days afloat sitting in a chair on the deck, seeking to make sense of the material Henry provided.

Those books and papers appeared to be saying that the abolition movement in America had recently split into two separate camps. On the one side, William Lloyd Garrison and his friends held that because slavery was such an evil system, no individual who understood the difference between right and wrong could possibly support it. Thus if enough people could be aroused to express their opinion about slavery, the system would simply collapse. Exactly how this would occur, though, they could not say.

On the other hand, Mr. Birney and Henry and some other men thought Mr. Garrison could not succeed without paying more attention to politics. Unless men committed to ending slavery could be elected to Congress, they saw no prospect for a change of heart among Southern slaveowners. It was Henry's opinion that a new political party might have to be formed, having as the first point in its program the passage of new laws forbidding human slavery anywhere in the United States.

Although all through her girlhood Lizzie had sputtered about the way girls were expected to be less clever than boys, in one area she had followed the general pattern. Everybody seemed convinced that females had no business bothering their heads about politics. Who was running for President? What sort of new laws were being debated by Congress? Why should any girl take an interest in such questions when there was nothing she possibly could do about them?

Or rather, all she could do was to express her views to her father or her brothers or her husband. They could vote in elections, and otherwise take an active part in running the government, but apparently it had never struck anyone that women ought to have the same political rights the men in their families had. This thought had never even struck Lizzie.

For her own father had such very definite ideas concerning the proper place of girls and women. To him, it was beyond belief that any female could be so bold as to speak up even at home on any kind of political topic. Men had the duty of protecting females from all varieties of unpleasantness, including the noisy turmoil of election campaigns. And women had the duty of allowing men to do their political thinking for them. While Judge Cady had served a term in the House of Representatives in Washington during his younger days, he had naturally left his family home in Johnstown because the nation's capital at that time had been hardly more than a few splendid public buildings and some far less elegant boardinghouses, surrounded by mud and malarial swamps. The notion of discussing political affairs with his wife or daughters when he returned to his own fireside never so much as crossed his mind.

Thus Lizzie had had no practice in weighing political questions. When her new husband gave her his own opinion concerning the political aspects of the abolitionist controversy, she accepted it without wondering what other considerations might be involved. It was not just that Henry's viewpoint struck her as sensible; at this point in her life, she was extremely anxious to prove she could be a good wife. She enjoyed having Henry talk over his ideas with her, and she felt no impulse to doubt his superior wisdom. As a result, by the time the Stantons were nearing England, Lizzie thought of herself as a convinced supporter of the anti-Garrison faction of the abolitionists.

Toward the end of the trip, though, her excitement at being about to set foot on a foreign shore rose to such a pitch that she quite forgot the purpose of their journey. She stood by the deck's railing, peering ahead eagerly for her first sight of the British coastline. Then when the faint shadow of land on the horizon finally gave proof that they would soon be reaching the country of Shakespeare and Sir Walter Scott, the calm manner the new Mrs. Stanton had been trying to cultivate completely deserted her.

Just like the Lizzie of old, she ran to find Henry and show him what she had seen. When she discovered him in the salon, he was deep in conversation with Mr. Birney and one of the ship's officers. Not a bit aware of how she was upsetting Mr. Birney by rudely breaking into this discussion, she poured out her news. Then Henry, smiling in spite of her bad manners because she did look so pretty with such pink cheeks, told her another piece of news.

She would have to be patient a little longer, he explained, for the captain had decided they could not possibly approach much closer to the coast till the breeze freshened.

How long were they likely to remain helpless this way?

The ship's officer shrugged. He had known the wind to change with hardly an instant's warning, and he had known it to take several days.

An answer of this sort could scarcely satisfy Lizzie in her present mood. Hurrying out onto the deck, as if merely by watching the land on the horizon she could make the wind blow them there, she was one of the first passengers to see a small pilot boat coming toward them.

When it drew up alongside the larger vessel, its skipper shouted an offer to bring anyone ashore within six hours. Lizzie ran back to the salon. Her blue eyes were gleaming so brightly that her husband could not help but agree to her plan, and even Mr. Birney said he would join them.

Accordingly, one at a time, each of them was strapped into a sort of armchair and lowered to the pilot boat. Lizzie found this mode of transport positively thrilling, but terrifying too. After their baggage had been dropped down to them in a large net, she breathed more easily, though, and when they began skimming toward the shore she gaily congratulated herself.

For there did appear to be sufficient breeze to carry this lighter craft along—at least until they had sailed some two miles. Then the wind utterly died down. Unless they wished to bob around aimlessly all night, their skipper told them, someone would have to help him row toward the harbor.

So Henry took up an oar, with a pained glance at his bride. Soon it started turning dark, but he and the pilot doggedly rowed on while Mr. Birney kept muttering, "The woman tempted me, and I did leave the good ship." As for Lizzie, she tried to seem invisible. However, aside from Henry's sore hands and aching back, they were no worse for their adventure when they finally tied up at a splintery dock around midnight.

The next morning, even Henry forgave his wife in the cheery light of a perfect June day. Every notion they had ever had about how wonderfully quaint a British town should be seemed no more than the simple truth as they climbed on top of a coach in the courtyard of the inn where they had slept briefly but soundly under the puffiest quilts imaginable. The jaunty driver's brisk crack of his whip, the postman blowing merrily on his horn as he raced up to deliver the mail for London—every new sight and sound enchanted Lizzie.

Then after they clattered off on the high road, riding by roses red beyond belief in every doorway, then green fields of the deepest green she had ever seen, Lizzie's spirits soared higher and higher. Passing cottages and castles that belonged in a storybook, she would have been hardly surprised to see a knight in armor gallop up to their coach, or a beautiful princess on a pure white horse. Henry, and even Mr. Birney, kept smiling at her excited comments.

But London, when they at last reached the great city, struck her as rather a disappointment. How drab its streets looked in comparison with the glorious countryside! Still, she had to admit that she might be just too tired now to appreciate any new wonders. When they drew up at the dreary brick house on Queen Street where they had engaged lodgings, her main concern was to find a comfortable bed as quickly as possible.

By the following morning, Lizzie felt more ready for exploring, so immediately after breakfast she and Henry set out on foot to observe what they could of the world's largest city. Since their meeting would not start for another week, she hoped to inspect the famous landmarks of London before settling down to listen to speeches. Certainly she saw no reason for lingering at their boardinghouse, which still struck her as one of the gloomiest buildings she had ever come upon.

However, when they returned toward evening Lizzie

was surprised and pleased to hear that a party of ladies from Boston and Philadelphia had just arrived. They, too, would be attending the antislavery convention. No sooner had she gathered this interesting fact than she cast an inquiring look at her husband. Why had he not told her that there were to be some women delegates? As far as she had known, the only females taking any part in the meeting would be mere spectators like herself.

From the way Henry carefully avoided her eye, Lizzie could sense that here was a mystery she would have to investigate. Doing so proved not to be very difficult. Entering the parlor to await dinner, they found the new arrivals already seated there. Impulsively, Lizzie walked up to introduce herself.

While each of the dozen ladies in the group greeted her politely, Lizzie felt that she had in some way offended them. Most of them seemed old enough to be her mother, and by their garb she could see that many were of the Quaker faith. Had she shocked these gentle women by her forward manner?

No, she really did not think that could be the case. Then as Lizzie stood in some confusion, trying to understand what she had done wrong, one of the Quaker ladies smiled at her reassuringly. "I would be pleased if thee would sit beside me at dinner, my dear," Mrs. Lucretia Mott said, and took her arm.

As the doors to the dining room were flung open at that moment, Lizzie gratefully started toward the table with this sweet-faced woman. From the corner of her eye, she noted Henry talking to some Baptist ministers who were also staying in the house. Like Henry himself, they were leaders of the anti-Garrison wing of the American abolitionists.

Suddenly, Lizzie's quick mind caught a possible solution to the mystery. Suppose these women were all supporters of Mr. Garrison! That would explain why Henry failed to mention them, and why at least some of the ladies were assuming that Mrs. Stanton must be a sort of enemy.

But not till the conversation around the long table was opened by a minister who reminded Lizzie of her own father did she begin to gather the whole truth. Another issue quite apart from politics apparently divided the abolition movement. Mr. Garrison felt that women should be allowed to take an active part in the antislavery cause—and her own husband did not!

Lizzie gasped aloud as she realized this must be the case. For, in a cutting tone of voice, the minister was addressing Mrs. Mott. He had rather hoped she would have been satisfied to set America's abolitionists by the ears with her speech-making in public, he told her. But now he learned that she proposed to do the same thing in England.

"So woman's rights is to be the big issue here!"

The words escaped from Lizzie before she was even aware that she had opened her mouth. Across the table, Henry Stanton stared at her uneasily but she did not notice. For she herself was staring with amazed and admiring eyes at the gray-haired Mrs. Mott right beside her. And that Quaker lady, on discovering this young woman's deep feeling on a subject so close to her own heart, gave Lizzie a look of understanding she never forgot.

From then on, Lizzie seized every possible opportunity to sit with Mrs. Mott, asking questions and confiding in her. These two sat talking together in the lobby of the British Museum, while others among the American visitors gazed at case after case of objects left in England by the ancient Romans. Mrs. Mott and Mrs. Stanton drank tea together while their friends viewed the London prison where many famous figures of the past had been held behind bars.

As far as Lizzie Stanton was concerned, nothing that had ever happened in the past was nearly as important as the matters she and Lucretia Mott discussed. Despite the difference in their ages, they felt a sympathy that made them seem like sisters. It distressed Lizzie that she had somehow missed learning before that Mrs. Mott, down in Philadelphia, had already done great work for the cause of women by playing an active role in the abolitionist movement there, so active that her safety had repeatedly been threatened by rioters. At the same time, it clearly did more than just please Mrs. Mott to find a woman, young enough to have been one of her own daughters, as eager as Lizzie was to see women granted a new freedom.

Lizzie's joy in making this new acquaintance was increased still more by finding that Lucretia's husband fully approved of her activities. James Mott was a sturdy gentleman who earned a good living for his family by selling woolen material at his Philadelphia store. His own belief in the antislavery cause made him approve of the abolitionist movement, but being a quiet sort of man, he was glad to let Lucretia do most of the talking for them both. Now that their children no longer needed her at home, she had willingly agreed to become one of Mr. Garrison's representatives in London. James had not only raised no objection, he had so arranged his business affairs that he could come along with her.

And why not? Lizzie thought this was a splendid example of the way two married people could really be partners. Instead of having the wife be obliged to stay behind the scenes while the husband made all the important decisions and did all the important work, why should they not each do their share? If a wife had some interest or talent that led her outside her own home, why should she not be permitted to do as she wished? Why, indeed?

Henry Stanton kept hearing these questions day after day, right up until the morning when the anti-slavery meeting was scheduled to start.

It was a sunny morning, and the narrow streets of old London were a striking mixture of brightness and shadows as they walked toward Freemasons' Hall on Drury Lane. Lizzie wondered whether this might not be an omen of what was going to happen during the next few hours. For two opposing forces were about to clash, and in her own mind there was no doubt now that one of these stood for light, the other for darkness.

During this past week, it had become absolutely clear that some of the men expected to keep Mrs. Mott and the rest of the American ladies from taking any real part in the convention. These women had been chosen as delegates by several organized groups of anti-slavery workers. Nevertheless, a move to deny them seats in the meeting hall would almost certainly be the first order of business.

But the women were not without friends. Unfortunately, Mr. Garrison's ship had been delayed, and he could not be present himself to fight for the rights of the female delegates. In his place, though, Mr. Wendell Phillips of Boston would stand up for them. And on which side would Mr. Henry Stanton speak? Even Lizzie herself could not say. Still, she felt some hope that all her efforts had not been wasted, and as they reached Drury Lane she smiled at him before leaving to walk on with Mrs. Mott and the other women.

Ahead, she could see a large crowd of men waiting for the hall's doors to be opened. At the women's approach, Lizzie thought she heard a buzz of alarm spread among all these sober gentlemen from England, America, and a few other countries. How silly! But what *was* to be done about the ladies?

The answer was not long in coming. As soon as the doors were unlocked, polite ushers began leading the gentlemen into the main body of the hall and, at the same time, the ladies were led to a separate area. Set apart by a curtain, they would be out of sight, but they still would be able to hear the proceedings.

Lizzie felt no surprise. An arrangement of this sort had been spoken of, and it would serve till Mr. Phillips made his appeal. Immediately after the opening prayer, he did so.

Peering through a crack in the curtain, Lizzie saw a man above middle height, with a manner that would not have seemed out of place in the House of Lords. In fact, the aristocratic Wendell Phillips was one of the most respected figures in the American abolition movement. Nobody stirred as he began to speak.

The convention's first task, he said, must be to prepare *a correct list* of the delegates. And on this list, there must appear the names of *all persons* representing any antislavery group.

Lizzie smiled happily. When he said "all persons," he meant the ladies must be counted too. But before she could enjoy the clever way Mr. Phillips had worded his request, half a dozen other men were on their feet. A great debate was starting.

"No!"

"Yes!"

The issue kept swaying back and forth. Should the ladies be counted, or should they not? Lizzie listened with the most intense interest, and then, when a very familiar voice asked permission to speak, she could hardly restrain her feelings. What would her Henry have to say on this matter of such extreme importance to her?

"Yes!" Her words had not been wasted. He had changed his mind, at least on this one point. Yet Lizzie's beaming smile of victory faded soon enough. When the chairman called for a vote on the issue, the other delegates by an overwhelming margin refused to welcome the women.

Then as soon as the vote had been tallied, the British chairman said to Mr. Phillips, "I hope, sir, as the question is now decided, that you will assure us we can proceed with one heart and one mind."

Lizzie Stanton sat forward confidently. She knew Mr. Phillips would do no such thing. How could he fail to defend the rights of women as vigorously as he would defend freedom for Negro slaves? But it seemed that Mr. Phillips felt differently.

"There is no unpleasant feeling in our minds," Wendell Phillips said without hesitating. *"I have no doubt the women will sit with as much interest behind the curtain as though the vote had been otherwise.* All we asked was an expression of opinion, and, having obtained it, we shall now act with the utmost cordiality."

Lizzie felt as if she had been burned with a bar of red-hot iron. How could the man be so cruel? Did he not see what his words meant? To him, it seemed a trifling matter that a woman like Mrs. Mott should be treated with such disrespect.

"It's time!" Lizzie Stanton sputtered. "It's time some demand is made for new liberties for women."

"I quite agree, my dear," Lucretia Mott answered her.

•5•

~~AND SENECA FALLS

BEFORE LEAVING LONDON, MRS. STANTON AND MRS. Mott made a promise to each other. At the earliest opportunity, they would call a meeting of their own, and they would speak up about this whole matter of woman's rights.

Why were girls kept from getting higher education?

Why did women have so much difficulty in finding work, if they had no husband or father to protect them and had to provide for themselves?

Why, if a woman did manage to earn some money— as a teacher, by sewing, or by writing storybooks at home—was she paid much less than a man would receive for similar efforts?

And why, if a woman married, did she have to become less than a person in the eyes of the law? Why did a married woman have no legal right to own property or to appear in court or even to leave her husband if he turned into a hopeless drunkard?

From all the hours she had spent in her father's

office, Lizzie Stanton had a long list of similar questions. As for Lucretia Mott, during her own life she
had learned from firsthand experience about many of
the ways females were made to feel inferior.

As a seventeen-year-old teacher, she had known how
it felt to be paid not a penny for her work at the same
Quaker school where male teachers received decent
salaries. She had suffered ridicule, even had rotten
eggs thrown at her, because she had dared to appear
on the platform at antislavery meetings. And it was
not only hoodlums who attacked her. Many law-abid-
ing men thought the spectacle of a woman putting
herself forward in that way was so offensive that they
had no hesitation about trying to drown out her words
with shouted insults.

As a Quaker minister—for the Quakers were suf-
ficiently open-minded as to allow women to become
ministers—Mrs. Mott had come to believe she had a
duty to oppose the evil of slavery. So she had gone
right ahead with her speechmaking. Yet she was by
nature a much milder person than Lizzie Stanton.

By herself, Mrs. Mott had never dreamed of chal-
lenging the whole established order that was keeping
women down. But her sound common sense and Lizzie's
fire made a good combination. Together, might they
not achieve what neither could have done alone?

Still, it took Lucretia Mott and Lizzie Stanton eight
years till they finally carried out the promise they made
each other in London.

For their paths separated as soon as the antislavery

Henry B. Stanton in his later years   *Courtesy Harper & Row*
(from Henry B. Stanton's *Random Recollections*,
published in 1887)

convention ended. Suddenly Mrs. Stanton found herself boarding a steamer with her husband, bound for
France. There followed six of the busiest and most
inspiring months she had ever spent, inspecting points
of interest that Henry wrote about in letters to various

newspapers. They went to the top and bottom of every-thing, from church spires to tunnels, before sailing home on the first steamship to make regular Atlantic crossings.

Then they bravely visited the small city of Johns-town in upper New York State.

Judge Cady's welcome was hardly as warm as Lizzie would have liked, but at least he seemed bent on mak-ing the best of his new son-in-law. Indeed, the Judge turned out to have a plan all arranged for Henry's future—and Henry accepted it.

So, to Lizzie's extreme joy, peace was restored among those she loved most. At the somewhat advanced age of thirty-six, Henry Stanton became a law student. In the office of his father-in-law, he began preparing for a new career—one that had always attracted him, he told his wife privately. Yet she did not even think of confiding that she, too, had once wanted to be a lawyer. An entirely different ambition now absorbed her.

Lizzie Stanton, no less than Lizzie Cady, was not the sort to sit back and calmly await any important event. The instant she found out that she was going to have a baby, she quite forgot about almost every other mat-ter that had ever interested her. What a miracle to become a mother! But how would she be able to care for an infant? Her ignorance in this department was positively appalling. However, she would make it her business to learn all there was to know, so she would be well prepared for her own new career.

"Oh, Lizzie!" Her sisters and her married friends

kept teasing her about the endless questions she asked. They thought she was being very comical to search for books about babies. When the time came, she would manage just fine, they assured her.

No! Lizzie Stanton was not going to follow any old-fashioned system of child rearing, she insisted. And she proved her point much sooner than even those who knew her would have believed possible. Right after she gave birth to a healthy little boy, she began arguing with the nurse hired to help her.

Watching the nurse wrap the baby tightly in long strips of material, Mrs. Stanton demanded, "Can you give me one good reason, nurse, why a child should be bandaged that way?"

"Yes," said the elderly woman, "I can give you a dozen."

"I only asked for one."

At that, the nurse paused to think. "Well," she said, "the bones of a newborn infant are soft, and unless you pin them up snugly there is danger of their falling apart."

Mrs. Stanton almost leaped out of bed at hearing words that struck her as absurd. Feeling rather tired, though, she contented herself with murmuring something about how remarkable it was that kittens and puppies had no such trouble. Within the next few days, however, she made certain her son was allowed the freedom she was sure would be much better for him.

Thus although the boy was named Daniel Cady Stanton, after his strict grandfather, it astonished nobody when he developed into a lively young rascal. Neil, as they called him, was climbing out onto rooftops almost before he could walk. During the next few years his mother also had to cope with a baby Henry, and another son named Gerrit Smith Stanton in honor of the cousin who had introduced his parents to each other. Young Gat seemed even more adventurous than his brothers.

By this time the Stantons had moved from Johnstown to Boston, where the father of the family attempted to set up a law practice. Having so many mouths to feed might have caused some men to look for clients well able to pay fat fees, but Henry Stanton could not resist working for reformers who had hardly any money. While his wife loved him the more because he refused to turn down his old friends, certain problems soon arose.

Lizzie had chosen a charming little house, and she had never been happier. As a change from chasing after her young sons, she would leave them several times a week in charge of their nursemaid. She also had a cook to prepare the family's meals. For there was so much of interest going on in Boston, so many fascinating people. Since her husband already had a wide acquaintance among the city's leading figures, she became friendly with John Greenleaf Whittier, the well-known poet. Mr. Charles Sumner, who was plan-

ning to run for the United States Senate, came to
dinner. Mr. Stanton enjoyed playing host just as much
as Mrs. Stanton relished her own new role as hostess.
However, this pleasant style of living cost far more than
Henry Stanton earned.

As a result, unpaid bills began piling up. Mr. Stanton began to feel mysterious pains in his chest, and
Mrs. Stanton wondered if money worries might not be
the cause of his distress. At last she wrote to her father,
asking him for help.

Then Judge Cady angrily summoned the Stantons
back to Johnstown. Behind the closed door of his office
he gave a grim lecture to his son-in-law. Exactly what
words were spoken during this interview Lizzie never
learned. She stood tapping her foot impatiently till the
two men emerged.

Her husband rushed right past her, muttering that
he wanted to take a walk by himself. Meanwhile her
father gave his answer to her request.

Because Judge Cady was a man with a substantial
amount of property, he had long ago informed his
daughters that they would receive equal shares after
his death. Knowing this, Lizzie had hoped he might
give her at least part of her share immediately. Now
he told her that he would do so—in his own way.

On the outskirts of a country village about a hundred
miles west of Johnstown, in the rural heart of New
York State far from any city, he owned an abandoned
house. This property Elizabeth could have. It would
provide perfectly adequate and healthful surroundings

for bringing up his grandsons after some necessary repairs had been made. In a tone of mixed harshness and affection, the Judge said to his daughter, "You believe in woman's ability to do and dare. Now go ahead and put your place in order." With that, he handed her a check to pay the expenses of fixing up the neglected building and grounds.

In short, if she wished any help from him she would have to give up Boston's excitement. She would have to settle in the village of Seneca Falls. But what about Henry?

Henry Stanton knew just why the Judge had come to this decision. While they had been alone together, his father-in-law had made it clear that Boston in his eyes was a particularly unsuitable place to live. Not only was its east wind a dangerous cause of sickness, but its seething currents of new ideas were even more dangerous to mental stability. Judge Cady wanted no daughter of his exposed to this unhealthful climate. Elizabeth, especially, with her habit of taking up odd notions, would be much safer in Seneca Falls.

As for the husband Elizabeth had seen fit to select, Judge Cady would, of course, not presume to dictate any other man's conduct. However, it would surely seem to do any man more credit if he took his responsibilities to his wife and children seriously. Surely a quiet law practice in a decent community like Seneca Falls would make for more true happiness than all the noise of Boston.

Surely not! Henry Stanton could not for an instant

imagine spending the rest of his life in an isolated country village. He simply had to stay in close touch with the great events of the day. Already his name was widely known, and he thought he was not flattering himself to believe an even greater fame might be in store for him. He had proved he could speak and write effectively. The idea of taking an active part in politics attracted him more and more. How could he bury himself in sleepy Seneca Falls?

Yet he had a wife and sons to support. He had debts that must be paid. If he should take Judge Cady's advice, his financial burden would certainly be lighter. Suppose, though, that Lizzie and the boys went to Seneca Falls, while he himself resumed his newspaper writing? Then he would be able to spend weeks at a time in New York City or Washington. As a refreshing change from these busy cities, he would thoroughly enjoy visiting his family in the country. The more Henry Stanton mused about this plan, the better he liked it. In a much calmer frame of mind, he walked back to find Lizzie and tell her what he had decided.

She was less than delighted by his scheme. Still, she believed almost as firmly as he did that Henry Stanton deserved fame. Loving him well enough to put his welfare above her own, she agreed to go on to Seneca Falls alone. While one of her sisters tended her boys, and while Henry journeyed down to New York City to arrange for taking up his writing again, she energetically set about getting her old house repaired.

Her first sight of it nearly made her weep. On a muddy road away from the center of the village, without a single neighbor in hailing distance, it gave no hint of being worth saving. Its chimney had toppled, its yard was a tangle of weeds.

After she had got various handymen to hammer and paint and cut away dead branches, the effect was somewhat improved. Then when Henry appeared with the boys, and congratulated her on her efforts, she felt more hopeful. Once he departed, though, her spirits began sinking rapidly.

For several months she did try to find the bright side of her new situation. Halfway measures could never suit her, and so she flung herself into domestic tasks like preserving strawberries and collecting recipes for pickles. Now that she was living in the country, she told herself, the least she could do was to win some blue ribbons at the county fair. Yet she could not help arguing with herself.

How was she to escape being bored to death by the humdrum routine of this new life? In isolated Seneca Falls, having a hired girl to help with housekeeping chores failed to give her any real freedom. How was she to use her spare energy and her very real abilities? Although she adored her boys, they drove her all but out of her mind by their mischief when she had to stay with them all day long. Standing over a hot stove in July, stirring kettles of boiling fruit juices, could not really satisfy her urge to do something on her own that was interesting and worth doing. Before a year had passed, she had begun to feel as if her brain itself was turning into jelly.

Not being particularly good at keeping secrets, Mrs. Stanton could not help letting her husband know what was going on inside her. So during his long absences he did all he could think of to make her happier. He sent her one parcel after another of reading material—newspapers and pamphlets and books—and he told her that if she could keep up with this flood, she would be better informed about current issues than any city dweller.

At first this plan worked wonders. Having reason to walk into town frequently and stop at the post office, Mrs. Stanton became more friendly with some of her new neighbors. On closer acquaintance, she found they were perfectly nice people, neither as prim nor as ignorant as she had assumed. Once she had dropped the superior air of a recent resident of Boston, a real friendship developed between her and the red-haired postmistress, Mrs. Amelia Bloomer.

Soon Mrs. Stanton and Mrs. Bloomer were both reading the papers Henry Stanton sent. They had long talks about the slavery question, even about politics. It made Lizzie feel rather pleased to be able to confide that James Birney, the candidate for President of the United States put up by the abolitionists, was the same Mr. Birney who had traveled to England with her.

But Lizzie Stanton's discontent came back in full force whenever her husband returned to Seneca Falls— or rather, when he packed up to leave again after one of his visits. While he was home, she felt marvelously alive and cheerful. It did her heart good to see him tossing Gat up in the air, or playing ball with the older boys. Then she could believe that their marriage was the kind of partnership she had hoped it would be. Yet no sooner did Henry depart than her doubts began again.

Why had she even bothered to learn how to read? Who cared that she knew as much on many subjects as most men did? While her husband was out making his mark in the great world, why must the kitchen and the nursery remain the boundaries of her world?

Then, in the spring of 1848, she received a letter that raised a new question in her mind. Henry wrote to give her some splendid news from his point of view. He had just been asked to run for the New York State Legislature, and he stood a fair chance of winning.

Suddenly Lizzie Stanton's patience snapped. How could she bear this added unfairness of not being able to cast a vote for her own husband?

Nearly eight years had passed since she had parted with Lucretia Mott in London. During this period they had stayed in touch by mail, but Mrs. Mott's antislavery work had been keeping her on the move. No opportunity for planning their women's rights meeting had presented itself. Now Mrs. Stanton made up her mind they must not wait any longer. She picked up a pen and begged her old friend to consider visiting her.

When she sent her appeal, Mrs. Stanton knew that a married sister of Lucretia's had settled not far from Seneca Falls. She hoped this family connection would provide another reason for Mrs. Mott to make the trip. It so happened there was a third reason, one that Mrs. Stanton could not have been aware of. After tirelessly traveling to abolitionist meetings month after month, James and Lucretia Mott were both feeling the need for a rest in the country.

Thus on a pleasant morning early that July, Lizzie Stanton was overjoyed to receive an invitation to a tea party at the home of a Mrs. Richard Hunt in nearby Auburn. Lucretia Mott had just arrived there!

Henry Stanton was spending that month with his family, but Lizzie did not hesitate about leaving him for the day. Giving him some hasty instructions about keeping Gat from climbing trees, she hitched a pony to their cart and drove off. While the pony trotted along, she thought of several ideas.

"How goes it with thee?" Lucretia Mott grasped Lizzie's hands and greeted her affectionately an hour later. Without even thinking about what the proper answer ought to be at a tea party, Lizzie immediately began to pour forth her plans.

They must hold the meeting they had spoken of in London, she said, and they must hold it right away, before Lucretia was obliged to leave the area.

Mrs. Mott gently protested. What could they possibly accomplish by calling a meeting in this rural area? Surely they should wait until they could both arrange to be in some major city.

No! Lizzie Stanton shook her head. They had waited long enough already.

But who would attend such a meeting in Seneca Falls?

Women from every town for miles around, and farm wives and daughters, too.

Farm wives would come at the height of the haying season?

Indeed they would!

Smiling as she realized that her friend had not grown any less impulsive since becoming a mother, Lucretia Mott stopped raising objections. Perhaps they really might plant some small seed, she thought, remembering how several new religious movements and other reform waves had gotten their start in this same area of central New York State.

Meanwhile Lizzie had borrowed a pen and paper from her hostess. Bending over the tea table, she wrote a paragraph that appeared on July 14, 1848, in the *Seneca County Courier*:

> WOMAN'S RIGHTS CONVENTION—A Convention to discuss the social, civil, and religious condition and rights of women, will be held in the Wesleyan Chapel at Seneca Falls, N.Y., on Wednesday and Thursday, the 19th and 20th of July, current, commencing at 10 o'clock A.M. The public generally are invited to be present . . . Lucretia Mott of Philadelphia, and other ladies and gentlemen will address the Convention.

Only after she had finished writing this did Lizzie Stanton agree to sit down with the other ladies and drink a cup of tea.

Still, she could not feel at ease. The convention was less than a week off, and some sort of program had to be arranged. A statement of purpose had to be prepared. Fortunately, four or five of the other ladies seemed eager to take part in the planning, and they agreed to meet again the following day.

Sitting around a sturdy table in Mrs. Martha Wright's parlor the next day, they listened as Lizzie Stanton insisted on the need to take some dramatic step. Suppose, she said, some document famous in American history were used as their model—like the Declaration of Independence, with its list of oppressions suffered by all Americans under the rule of King George. And suppose it were rewritten, to list the oppressions suffered by all women under the harsh rule of men.

"When, in the course of human events . . ." Mrs. Stanton's pen raced across a page of paper. "We hold these truths to be self-evident: that all men *and women* are created equal . . ."

For several minutes the other ladies nodded with approval as Mrs. Stanton went on to list many of the ways in which women were treated unfairly. But all at once there were puzzled looks. A gasp of surprise sounded. Mrs. Stanton appeared to be saying that one basic right belonged as much to women as to men, the right to vote. Even Lucretia Mott stared in amazement.

"Why, Lizzie," she said, "thee will make us ridiculous!"

Henry Stanton quite agreed with Mrs. Mott. That

evening, listening to his wife read the statement she had prepared, he pulled hard at his mustache when she reached this same point. If she proposed to make a fool of herself by coming out with such nonsense in public, he could not stop her, he muttered. But he would not stay to hear her, either. Unless she changed her speech, he would leave town till her meeting ended.

Why? Did he not wish women to vote for him?

Certainly not! Any man who favored such a radical notion could never win any election. So would she please consider his wishes and omit this portion of her statement?

No, she could not! Without the right to vote, even the best-educated woman in the country would still be inferior to the most ignorant man.

So Henry Stanton was not among those present three days later when his wife stood up in front of a larger audience than even she had expected. About three hundred women and a few dozen men had come to this meeting, mainly because they were curious about Mrs. Lucretia Mott. From her constant speaking in the anti-slavery cause, Mrs. Mott had become widely known.

Until Lizzie Stanton stepped forward that morning and in a clear voice read out her Declaration of Independence, nobody beyond her own immediate circle had ever heard of her. From then on, though, a lot of other people began to hear of Elizabeth Cady Stanton.

BLOOMERS AND SUSAN

HER FIRST TASTE OF PUBLIC LIFE THRILLED MRS. STAN-
ton. Though shocked murmurs greeted her demand for
the right to vote, the rest of her statement struck most
of her audience as reasonable. For this was a reform-
minded group, as might be expected, considering that
Mrs. Mott had been the magnet which had drawn them
to Seneca Falls. It was an open-minded group, too.

At the end of two days of debate, sixty-eight women
and thirty-two men walked forward to sign Mrs. Stanton's Declaration.

Yet Lucretia Mott and Henry Stanton had both been
quite right about what the reaction of the public at
large would be. The few newspapers that thought the
women's meeting was worth mentioning treated it as a
great joke.

PROGRESS?

That was the headline one editor put on his story,
and then he wrote:

The women folks have just held a Convention up in N.Y. State, and passed a sort of 'bill of rights' affirming it their right to vote, to be teachers, legislators, lawyers, divines, and do all the sundries the 'lords' may, and of right do now. They should have resolved at the same time that it was obligatory on the 'lords' aforesaid, to wash dishes, handle the broom, darn stockings, scold the servants, dress in the latest fashion . . . and be as fascinating as these blessed morsels of humanity whom God gave us to preserve that rough animal man, in something like reasonable civilization. Progress! Progress forever!

Lizzie Stanton did not in the least mind having fun poked at her program. Let people laugh, she told her husband airily. Soon enough they would come to realize this matter of woman's rights had to be taken seriously.

Why, the whole world was bubbling with new ideas, she pointed out. Over in Europe, one tyrant after another was being toppled from power. Right here in the United States, new steam engines and new factories were shaking the nation out of its old ways. The liberation of women was bound to come as a result of all this upheaval.

For his part, Henry Stanton remained more concerned with other questions. Politics, and especially the success of the new antislavery party calling itself Free Soil Democrats—these were his most absorbing interests. After he did win a seat in the state legislature, he put even canal building above his wife's cause.

Yet now that she had a cause to absorb her own

mind, Mrs. Stanton felt much happier. While she sewed shirts or shaped piecrusts, she never stopped thinking of how to improve the lot of women everywhere. Nor did she keep her thoughts to herself.

From the very day she made her Declaration, she no longer could doubt that she had important work to do. When farm wives told her with tears in their eyes that they wanted to thank her for saying what they had often thought themselves, but had never been able to put into words, Lizzie Stanton stopped wondering why she had ever learned to read and write. When other women over in Rochester, New York, then even in Ohio held similar meetings, she could not accept their invitations to attend. However, she could—and did—write stirring words of encouragement that were read for her at those meetings.

What was more, she found a fine new method of expressing herself right in Seneca Falls. Her friend Mrs. Bloomer, needing a little extra money, started a small paper appealing to women readers, and Mrs. Stanton cheerfully gave her a long article every week. Mrs. Bloomer called her paper *The Lily,* for her ideas were rather less advanced than Lizzie Stanton's. To Mrs. Bloomer, this white flower was a perfect symbol of the pure, old-fashioned virtues all females should aim to represent.

Instead of debating with her friend, Mrs. Stanton played a sly game of her own. Having learned quite a bit about gardening since moving to the country, she knew there was one flower nobody could fail to notice because it grew so fast and produced such a number of huge golden blossoms. Thus, when she handed in a piece of her writing she always signed it "Sunflower."

And what she wrote was just as attention-getting as the symbol she had selected. For instance, under the innocent heading "Sewing," Mrs. Stanton had this to say:

> As an amusement, it is contemptible; as an educator of head or heart, worthless; as a developer of muscle, of no avail; as a support, the most miserable of trades. It is a continued drain on sight and strength, on health and life, and it should be the study of every woman to do as little of it as possible. . . .
>
> What use is all the flummering, puffing and mysterious folding we see in ladies' dresses? What use in ruffles on pillow cases, night caps, and children's clothes? What use in making shirts for our lords in the wonderful manner we do, with all those tiny plaits, and rows of stitching down before and round the collars and wrist bands?
>
> Why, all these things are done to make the men, women, children, chairs, sofas and tables look pretty? If the women for the last fifty years had spent all the time they have wasted in furbelowing their rags, on walking, riding, or playing on the lawn with their children, the whole race would look ten times as well as they do now!

Mrs. Stanton felt a healthy glow of satisfaction every time she tore away in this manner at some commonly accepted notion concerning females. Although Mrs. Bloomer disagreed with many of her friend's opinions, she saw no harm in printing them.

However, Mrs. Stanton had more on her mind than just tearing down old ways of doing things. She also wanted to win support for the new ways she believed in more deeply every day. So she boldly raised the question, "Why Must Women Vote?" And then, without even imagining that she might embarrass Mrs. Bloomer, she made a suggestion.

One of Lizzie Stanton's cousins had recently returned to the United States after a long stay abroad. The same Lib Smith at whose home Lizzie had met Henry Stanton was now Mrs. Charles Dudley Miller. On a Monday morning early in February of 1851, Mrs. Stanton wrote to Mrs. Miller:

> I have actually got my fourth son! Yes, Theodore Stanton bounded upon the stage of life with great ease —comparatively!! He weighs ten and one-half pounds. I was sick but a few hours. At seven o'clock Sunday morning he was born. This morning I got up, bathed myself in cold water, and am sitting by the table writing several letters.

Mrs. Miller found it hard to believe that even Lizzie could recover so quickly from giving birth to a baby, and she immediately set out for Seneca Falls. Because the weather was bad, she wore an unusual costume she had bought in distant Turkey. The minute Lizzie Stanton saw it, an idea flashed into her mind.

What incredible freedom not to have a long skirt trailing in the mud or snow! For Mrs. Miller was wearing a pair of wide black trousers, beneath a full skirt reaching only to the knee. A knee-length cloak trimmed with fur and a dashing beaver hat completed her outfit. Mrs. Stanton instantly decided to copy the whole costume.

No sooner had she done so than an even grander idea occurred to her. Why should this marvelous new freedom from long skirts not be shared by every woman? Quickly she prepared complete directions for making the necessary garments, and she delivered these to the editor of *The Lily*. All Mrs. Bloomer did was to print the information in her paper.

Thus it hardly seemed fair that, within the next few months, people all over the country were laughing at women wearing *bloomers*.

Even Lizzie Stanton's menfolk made fun of the new garb. Writing to her from Albany, when he had merely heard about the odd pantaloons, her husband asked her, "How does Lib Miller look in her new Turkish dress? The worst thing about it would be, I should think, sitting down. Then ladies will expose their legs somewhat above the knees, to the delight of those gentlemen who are curious about whether their lady friends have round and plump legs, or lean and scrawny ones."

But once Lizzie herself began appearing everywhere in trousers—during a period while he was running for

Mrs. Stanton in her bloomer costume, 1851
Courtesy Harper & Row
(from **Mrs.** Stanton's autobiography *Eighty Years and More,*
published in 1898)

election again—he took a less tolerant view. "Some good Democrats say they will not vote for a man whose wife wears bloomers," he informed her unhappily.

Then Mrs. Stanton's oldest son, who had recently been sent off to boarding school, wrote begging her not to wear trousers when she paid him a visit. But she replied:

Dear Neil,

You do not wish me to visit you in a short dress! Why, my dear child, I have no other. Now suppose you and I were taking a long walk in the fields and I had on three long petticoats. Then suppose a bull should take after us. Why, you, with your legs and arms free, could run like a shot; but I, alas! should fall a victim to my graceful flowing drapery. My petticoats would be caught by the stumps and the briars, and what could I do at the fences? Then you in your agony, when you saw the bull gaining on me, would say, "Oh! how I wish Mother could use her legs as I can." Now why do you wish me to wear what is uncomfortable, inconvenient, and many times dangerous? I'll tell you why. You want me to be like other people. You do not like to have me laughed at. You must learn not to care what foolish people say. Such good men as Cousin Gerrit will tell you that a short dress is the right kind. So no matter if silly ignorant persons do laugh. Good night to you; my dear boy.

Your Mother.

Mrs. Stanton put on just as brave a manner when she and Mrs. Miller dared to wear their unconventional attire while visiting relatives in New York City. She wrote assuring Mrs. Bloomer that "the talking about it being dangerous to walk the streets in the new costume is, as I told you, all humbug!" After several days of going everywhere, even to church, in their short dresses, they had been stared at, she admitted, but not otherwise treated unpleasantly. "We have been taken for Hungarians," she guessed.

Nevertheless, a good many of the other women who did follow her example had less happy experiences. Small boys, even grown men, hooted at them wherever they went. Day and night, they kept hearing this chant:

> Hi! Ho! In rain and snow,
> The bloomer now is all the go!

Finally, even Lizzie Stanton confessed in a letter to Lib Miller:

> Had I counted the cost of the short dress, I would never have put it on. However, I'll never take it off, for now it involves a principle of freedom. . . .
> I am often tired of this fight. How wearisome to be forever warding off attacks. Tonight I am ready to lay down my life, but oh! tomorrow the sun will shine and my blessed baby will open his sweet blue eyes, crow and look so lovingly on me that I shall live joyfully again.

When Mrs. Miller received this letter, another few words were scribbled at the bottom of the page: "Thursday morning. The sun is up, the baby has crowed and his mother feels happy."

However, after two years of stubbornly wearing only

short dresses, finally Mrs. Stanton decided she was using too much of her strength defending the new style. She began taking down her hems again, meanwhile grumbling to Mrs. Miller:

> For us commonplace, everyday, working characters who wash and iron, bake and brew, carry water and fat babies upstairs and down, bring potatoes, apples and pans of milk from the cellar, run our own errands through mud and snow, shovel paths and work in the garden, why the 'drapery' is quite too much. One might as well work with a ball and chain.

But she was feeling far more cheerful than she sounded. For she had just had the great good fortune of making the acquaintance of Miss Susan Brownell Anthony.

Lizzie Stanton never forgot the first moment she saw Susan—because she did forget something else. It was a warm summer afternoon, and she had left her mischief-loving boys home with only an addle-headed hired girl to mind them. William Lloyd Garrison himself was speaking at an abolitionist meeting in Seneca Falls, and Mrs. Stanton could not bear to miss such an occasion.

Indeed, she even invited Mr. Garrison home to dinner, despite the danger of finding that her wild Indians had set fire to the house in her absence. Then, as they were walking back together, Mrs. Bloomer stopped them to introduce a teacher from Rochester who had come over for a few days.

Mrs. Stanton decided at one glance that she liked this young woman. Dressed all in gray, except for the blue ribbons on her hat, Miss Anthony made a perfect picture of neatness. Her smile was warm, and she appeared to be extremely well-informed. As they stood chatting, it was on the tip of Lizzie Stanton's tongue to ask Miss Anthony to join them for dinner. All at once, though, she remembered about her boys, and she hurriedly led Mr. Garrison away without any further ceremony.

She and Susan laughed over this many times afterward. For it turned out that Miss Anthony had been hoping for the very invitation Mrs. Stanton had been tempted to offer. She had already heard of Elizabeth Cady Stanton, she had read some of her writings, and she admired her enormously.

But no real harm was done by Mrs. Stanton's omission. Within a few years Susan B., as the Stanton children called her, had become a regular visitor in Seneca Falls, and one of the most notable friendships in all of American history had begun making headlines. As Henry Stanton dryly put it to his wife, "You stir up Susan, and she stirs up the world."

Although Lucretia Mott was still the guiding spirit of the woman's rights movement, her advancing age kept her from taking much part in its work. Fortunately a number of younger women like Lucy Stone were devoting their energy to the cause. However, the hard task of forcing the public to pay some attention to the woman question fell largely to Mrs. Stanton and Miss Anthony.

Each had her own special talents. One was forever thinking of new ideas, while the other's strong point was the ability to act. So they made a good team.

Actually, Susan Anthony had started her own career as a reformer by concentrating on a different issue. Soon after becoming the director of the girls' department of a private academy, she had attended a dance with a young man. During the course of the evening he drank more than he should have, and his behavior disgusted her.

"My fancy for attending dances is fully satisfied," she wrote in her diary. Instead, she started spending all her spare time helping to form a new organization. It was called the Daughters of Temperance, and its aim was to discourage the use of strong drink.

After just a few months, Miss Anthony proved that she had a rare gift. Like a general in command of an army, she could plan a campaign down to the smallest detail. She found ways to enlist new members, she raised money, she arranged meetings.

But even when she succeeded in making the Daughters an effective fighting force, the men who had formed the Sons of Temperance were not impressed. A small group of women was allowed to attend a statewide convention planned by the men. However, the minute Miss Anthony rose to ask a question, she was shouted down. Rapping for silence, the chairman coldly told her that female delegates had been admitted merely to *listen and learn.*

Susan Anthony strode out of that meeting hall feeling exactly as Lizzie Stanton had felt ten years earlier in London, when women delegates had been forbidden to take any part in the antislavery conference there.

So the woman's rights movement was closely related to the two other leading reform movements of the nineteenth century. Possibly Lizzie Stanton might have devoted her efforts to the antislavery cause, and Susan Anthony might have spent her life working for temperance, if they had been permitted to pour all their energy into those channels. They both continued to support the aims of the other movements, as did many of their followers. Yet they could not help feeling that full equality for females had to come first.

As a result, they forged a close bond during the 1850's. Five years younger than Mrs. Stanton, Susan Anthony looked up to her—she never dreamed of calling her by her first name. Yet Susan B.'s sound good sense provided just the necessary balance to prevent her more brilliant friend from flying off on too many side issues.

Even their personal lives helped to further their purpose. After they began working together, Mrs. Stanton had three more babies—two little girls at last, and then another son. By now a marvelously capable Quaker widow named Mrs. Willard had moved into her household to assist her with domestic duties. However, only frequent visits from Susan B. kept woman's rights alive in those years.

"Men and angels, give me patience!" Mrs. Stanton exploded in one of her frequent letters to Miss Anthony. "I am at the boiling point! Oh, Susan! Susan! Susan! You must manage to spend a week with me before the Rochester convention."

So a few weeks later, while Susan bravely rescued baby Hattie from being shot with a bow and arrow by one of her brothers, Hattie's mother sat frowning over a heap of papers. And by evening, the full program for the Rochester meeting had been planned.

Having no family responsibilities of her own, Miss Anthony enjoyed her visits to Seneca Falls hugely. They gave her a taste of motherhood that she would otherwise have missed, and at the same time they relieved her friend from feeling too heavily burdened. In fact, their whole partnership involved a similar division of labor.

Since Mrs. Stanton could only rarely leave Seneca Falls, Miss Anthony would spend weeks on end traveling around the state, circulating petitions and arranging meetings. Then one day she would stride across the Stanton lawn, carrying a suitcase stuffed with scribbled notes, newspaper clippings, and other material about the woman question.

For Susan B. hated having to write a speech or report. She said she might as well try walking on stilts as to pick up a pen and compose anything sensible. Mrs.

Stanton, on the other hand, found writing as easy as breathing, so she would cheerfully prepare all the documents Susan required.

Then they would consult together about what their strategy should be during the coming months. And then Susan would set out again, with a stack of new petitions under her arm or some other plan in mind for stirring up the men of America.

One man in particular was aroused by one of these plans. Yet Judge Cady had himself been the inspiration for this scheme. In the summer of 1854, while Susan was visiting Seneca Falls, Mrs. Stanton happened to recall an incident from her own girlhood. As they sat on the porch sipping lemonade, she told about how she had once planned to take a scissors and simply cut all the unfair laws out of her father's books. She also remembered exactly what the Judge had told her then:

"When you are grown up and able to prepare a speech, you might go down to Albany and talk to the lawmakers there. Tell them all you have seen in this office—the sufferings of poor women deprived of their legal rights—and if you can persuade these men to pass new laws, the old ones will be dead letters."

Now Lizzie Stanton was nearly forty. She had become rather plump, and her hair was starting to turn gray. Nobody could doubt that she was grown up, and she certainly knew how to prepare a speech. Suddenly her eyes sparkled with glee.

Why not try it?

Why not go to Albany, as her father had suggested

long ago? Instead of merely sending stacks of petitions to the lawmakers, why not address those men in person?

But Susan looked doubtful. No woman had ever been allowed to speak before any such official body. What if they refused to listen?

Mrs. Stanton, though, was carried away by enthusiasm. The fact that her husband had recently given up his office and was once more writing from Washington and New York may have made her bolder. Wouldn't he be astonished to read about another member of the family making a splash in Albany!

If Henry Stanton was startled, Judge Cady was more so. When he saw a note in the *Albany Evening Journal* to the effect that his own daughter was planning to speak in the capitol, he wrote requesting her to stop off in Johnstown first. All at once, Mrs. Stanton felt like a little girl again.

Still, she could not possibly back down. Arrangements of every description had already been made for her appearance. A committee of lawmakers had even agreed to hear her. Susan, having fallen into the spirit of the adventure, had planned a convention of women from every part of the state to meet in Albany at the same time Mrs. Stanton was making her presentation. Petitions signed by thousands of other women—and some men, too—would be handed to the legislature. Complicated measures to ensure the well-being of the Stanton children while their mother was giving her speech had been set in motion. The speech itself was already written.

Yet Lizzie Stanton had never in her life trembled

more than she did as she started to read her speech in Johnstown to an audience of just one person.

"To the Legislature of the State of New York," she began in a faltering tone.

"The thinking minds of all nations call for change. There is a deep-lying struggle in the whole fabric of society, a grinding collision of the New with the Old . . ."

Her father listened to her without saying a word. Gradually she felt more confident and began reading in a stronger voice, describing many different cases where women were treated unfairly by one law or another.

When she finished at last, Judge Cady still remained silent. But the expression on his face gave her reason to hope she had touched his heart. Finally he spoke.

"Surely you have had a happy, comfortable life, with all your wants and needs supplied," he said. "And yet that speech fills me with self-reproach. For one might naturally ask, how can a young woman, tenderly brought up, who has had no bitter personal experience, feel so keenly the wrongs of her sex. Where did you learn this lesson?"

Lizzie Stanton answered him quietly. "I learned it here, in your office, when I was a child and I listened to the complaints made to you."

"Well, well!" The Judge shook his head. Then as had happened so often in the past, he gazed at her with mixed pride and sadness. "You have made your points clear and strong," he told her. "But I think I can find you even more cruel laws than those you have quoted."

So Judge Cady and his daughter sat up together till after midnight, turning the pages of his law books. When they finished, he kissed her on the forehead and then took his candle to go up to bed. After that evening, he never again criticized the work she was doing.

And after that evening, standing up in front of a committee of lawmakers was almost easy. For more than an hour Mrs. Elizabeth Cady Stanton spoke forcefully, championing women's rights—to own property, to earn their living, even to vote.

No woman had ever before even been given a chance to make such an appeal. On this first occasion, Mrs. Stanton was treated politely. None of the men present laughed at her or made any rude comments. Yet when the committee's chairman rose the following day to read the group's views about the serious questions she had raised, and about the petitions she had handed in, the ladies in the audience felt as if they would have preferred mere laughter. For that report dismissed her entire case with chilling scorn. It ended:

> On the whole, the Committee have concluded to recommend no measure, except as they have observed several instances in which husband and wife have signed the same petition. In such case, we would recommend the parties to apply for a law authorizing them to change dress, that the husband may wear the petticoats and the wife the breeches, and thus indicate to their neighbors and the public the true relation in which they stand to each other.

•7•

THE NEXT STEPS

NEVER MIND, MRS. STANTON SAID TO SUSAN. LAW-makers who ridiculed the uprising of women should really be pitied because they had heads about the size of an apple.

In the long run, Lizzie Stanton kept insisting, women were bound to win. Already they were accomplishing something important by making people pay attention to their cause. At least one famous editor was now on their side, even if his support was rather lukewarm. For Horace Greeley, in his *New York Tribune,* told his readers:

> It is easy to be smart, to be droll, to be facetious in opposition to these demands of female reformers. In decrying ideas so novel and so opposed to established habits and usages, a little wit will go a great way. But when a sincere republican is asked to say in sober earnestness what adequate reason he can give for refusing the demand of the women for an equal participation with men in political rights, he must answer—None.

Susan B. Anthony about 1850   *Library of Congress*

True, he may say that he believes it unwise in them to make the demand, but if they should generally prefer a complete political equality with men it is but the assertion of a natural right and so must be conceded.

Yet Mrs. Stanton herself had to admit that Mr. Greeley had put his finger on a sore point. By saying if women *generally* were to demand equality, the demand would have to be met, he was raising the basic question in her own mind: How could the majority of women be made to see that they must no longer accept the inferior place they had always been told they deserved?

For Mrs. Stanton could not fool herself. After several years of hard work, she had learned a sad lesson. Most women were still so fearful about offending their menfolk, or so uninterested in any matter beyond their personal concerns, that they refused to join their sisters in fighting for equal rights. Every time Susan returned to Seneca Falls, she brought new stories about doors being slammed in her face.

"I have all the rights I need!"

It was bad enough if a banker's wife whose days were all wasted on silly gossip said this as she refused to sign one of Susan's petitions. It was even worse when careworn workmen's wives, surrounded by sickly and ragged children, gave the same answer. While a few thousand thoughtful women were using their time and their talents to secure new opportunities for all females, by far the larger number simply turned their backs on the whole subject.

How Mrs. Stanton wished she could think of some way besides merely talking that would bring more women to their senses! Of course that would not solve the problem. Once the women of America were moved to demand equality, there would still remain the matter of convincing the nation's men. Only men could vote and pass new laws; the very same men who were depriving their wives and mothers and sisters of equal rights would have to give up their superior outlook, and to vote in favor of sharing their own privileges.

When Mrs. Stanton was feeling depressed, she would

fume about this absurd state of affairs. Why should men be allowed the sole right to judge women's claims for equality, any more than slaveowners should be allowed to decide all by themselves whether or not slavery should be permitted?

To Mrs. Stanton, there was a clear similarity between women and slaves. She was always willing to argue that although most women were treated better than most slaves were, actually they had the same status. Individuals belonging to either group were at the mercy of their masters, and were prevented from doing as they wished with their lives.

Nor was Mrs. Stanton alone in thinking along these lines. Her worst enemies often used almost her exact words. For instance, James Gordon Bennett, the editor of the *New York Herald,* wrote one day:

> How did woman first become subject to man, as she is now all over the world? By her nature, her sex, just as the Negro is and always will be to the end of time inferior to the white race and, therefore, doomed to subjection; *but she is happier than she would be in any other condition, just because it is the law of nature.*

Reading over that last sentence, Mrs. Stanton could hardly control her anger. Happier, indeed! Just let Mr. Bennett spend a few weeks scrubbing floors, or merely lacing himself up into a tight corset in order to appear properly slender, before he dared to assume that anybody enjoyed such occupations. No, that man was mistaken!

So Mrs. Stanton dashed off a letter to Susan. She

told her that holding more meetings might not accomplish much, but they must not stop now. While her babies were still small she could not leave them easily; thus, for the time being, Susan must do the arranging and the speaking too.

When Susan protested that she could not talk effectively in front of a large audience, Mrs. Stanton gave her no choice. "I have no doubt," she wrote, "that a little practice will make you an admirable lecturer." Then she added some specific advice:

> But you must dress loosely, take a great deal of exercise, and sleep enough. The body has a great influence on the mind. If you are attacked at your meetings, be good-natured and keep cool.

Satisfied that Susan would surely succeed by following this guidance, Mrs. Stanton spent most of the next few years concentrating on household problems. With her oldest boys approaching college age while their little sisters were still catching the measles, she faced a wide variety of domestic difficulties. Not long after the young Hattie and Maggie learned to say, "Mama," a different sort of language crisis arose.

Neil and Gat and Henry Jr.—he was called Kit in the family—were all home from school for the summer. Their mother tried for several weeks to make believe she had not noticed a new habit they had somehow picked up. At last, though, she had to face the truth. Her dear boys had taken to using swear words.

How could she teach them to stop? It happened that

Lucretia Mott was visiting again in the neighborhood, and she came to stay several days at the Stantons'. More than sixty years old now, her pure white hair and untroubled manner gave her a saintly look. However, she cheerfully agreed to the plan Lizzie Stanton suggested.

Whenever there was company in the Stanton house, the older children waited on the guests at the dinner table. Not only did this solve the problem of how to entertain constantly without a large staff of servants, but Mrs. Stanton also thought the task was good for her boys. She paid them for their work, and she expected them to take the job seriously.

Doing as he had been taught, Neil served the main course first to Mrs. Mott the evening she arrived. In her starched Quaker cap, she seemed the most prim and proper person imaginable. But after helping herself, she turned toward her hostess and asked, "May I give thee a piece of this damned chicken?"

Neil almost dropped the platter. Kit, coming after him with a dish of potatoes, gasped. He was sure his ears had played him some trick, yet Mrs. Mott repeated her question, so there could be no doubt about what she had said. And then during the rest of the meal their mother and Mrs. Mott and Susan B., who was also visiting, kept asking similar questions at every opportunity.

This strange performance continued for three days. On the fourth, a United States Senator who lived in the nearest city and several other highly respected

ladies and gentlemen also joined the party. Nobody
except the Stanton boys appeared to be shocked when
the hostess and her friends kept using language rarely
heard in polite society.

At last, Gat got his mother alone. With tears in his
eyes he demanded to know, "What will Senator Seward
and the others think of you, swearing like that?"

"Well," said Mrs. Stanton, "you boys all do it, and
so we thought we would. Don't you like to hear us?"

"Oh, no, Mother!" All three of the older boys spoke
up earnestly.

"Very well, then," Mrs. Stanton said, "if you boys
will stop swearing, I will also."

Not even realizing that they had been the victims of
one of their mother's little plots, her sons minded what
they said, at least in her presence, from that evening
onward.

Mrs. Stanton scored a number of other victories, too,
affecting other families in the area. She taught one
friend how to go about buying a new kitchen stove, even
though the woman's husband saw no need for giving
up the cranky dragon his wife had been struggling with
three times every day. She taught the wife of Senator
Seward to dare to speak up at home on the issue of
woman's rights. Then, as her babies grew older, she
resumed a more active role outside of her own community.

In fact, she decided to take up lecturing. People all
over the country seemed so hungry for a taste of cul-
ture that speakers on every sort of subject were being

sought by tour managers. Once Mrs. Stanton let it be known that she was willing to earn some money by talking on her favorite topic, she had no difficulty securing a series of engagements.

Her only difficulty—again—was with her father. During the preceding several years, their fondness for each other had overshadowed their differences of opinion. Writing to him to suggest that he get the new book *Uncle Tom's Cabin,* which she had found more affecting than any other volume she had ever read, she playfully signed herself, "Your affectionate but radical daughter." However, when she dropped some hints about her new plans, Judge Cady summoned her for a visit to Johnstown.

Asking her to come into the parlor after dinner, he solemnly inquired, "Elizabeth, are you getting ready to become a lecturer?"

"Yes, sir."

"Then I hope," he said, "that you will never do it in my lifetime, for if you do, be assured of one thing. Your first lecture will be a very expensive one."

"I intend that it shall be a very profitable one," she answered boldly.

At that the Judge took his candle and left the room by one door, while she took her candle and left by the other door. The next day, he carried out his threat and changed his will. Before she departed from Johnstown, Lizzie Stanton knew she could no longer expect to inherit any money when her father died.

Nevertheless, she went right ahead with her speaking. While she talked about woman's rights in several towns and cities, her husband was following a somewhat similar program. His topic, though, was the need for supporting the new Republican party, which had recently been formed by a number of different groups that were all strongly opposed to slavery.

In the late 1850's the slavery question was dividing the United States as no other issue had done since the birth of the nation. Even Mrs. Stanton, who was so deeply committed to her own cause, could see that all other matters must take a lesser place in the public's mind. Thus, after completing her first lecture tour, she returned with a heavy heart to Seneca Falls.

For now she fully shared her husband's dark mood about the future. When Henry had written to her from Washington and told her that a war between the states would surely break out shortly, she had refused to believe that men of good will could find no other solution. But in the course of her own travels she was shocked by the bitter words she heard concerning the South, and by the lack of any grounds for hope that bloodshed could be avoided.

Of course she felt strongly about slavery herself. Even before being married to an abolitionist, she had hated this evil system. She thought everybody, male or female, should be his or her own master. And her childhood love for old Abraham had given her the habit of disregarding the color of any person's skin. Since becoming active in the woman's rights cause, one of her most valued friends had been Frederick Douglass, a former slave whose powerful speaking on behalf of his own people did not prevent his warmly supporting Mrs. Stanton's work too. She never forgot that the antislavery newspaper he put out in Rochester had been the first journal anywhere to say a kind word about the movement she had started back in 1848.

So, ten years later, she could not help praying that if a war did start the North would win a swift victory. During the tense months while the country was being swept closer and closer toward open conflict, Mrs. Stanton became increasingly absorbed in politics. Would Senator Seward of New York, who had eaten so often at her dinner table, win sufficient support in the West to be nominated by the Republicans for President? Suppose Mr. Lincoln of Illinois got the top place on the new party's ticket? Could such a country bumpkin win the election, and if he did, could he be trusted to take a firm stand about slavery? How would a backwoods lawyer face the challenge of civil warfare if the South insisted on fighting?

But besides questions like these, Mrs. Stanton also had some difficult personal problems. In the spring of 1859, her father suddenly lost his eyesight. Although he was eighty years old, he had seemed as vigorous as many men far younger until he woke up blind one morning. Then within a few weeks he turned completely helpless.

His daughter had never suffered the way she did when she went to see him. Through her whole adult life she had been spared any close touch with serious illness—her own seven children were all blessedly strong and healthy, in a day when most large families knew the sadness of losing several infants. So her father's long struggle before he died that winter gave Mrs. Stanton her first experience of the pain of losing a loved relative.

At least, though, she had the peace of mind that came from knowing they had parted on good terms. After he sent for her, she spent countless hours during his last months sitting by his bed reading to him, or relieving her frail mother of other nursing chores. That her father had already had some second thoughts and had restored her name in his will hardly mattered to her, for she never fretted about money. That he did love her and feel proud of her, after all, mattered much more.

For how could money ease the new worry that kept nagging at her mind as 1860 opened a new decade? Each passing week made war seem more likely, and even in sleepy Seneca Falls troops of volunteer soldiers were starting to practice drilling. Her son Neil was eighteen; Kit was sixteen; Gat, still the most adventurous of all, was nearly fifteen. Naturally they wanted to join up, and their mother could scarcely blame them. Had she been a boy and their age, she would have felt exactly as they did. Yet suppose the worst came, and her precious sons went off to fight! How could she bear the horror of knowing they might be killed?

Then soon after the election that made Mr. Lincoln the President, Henry Stanton came up with a plan that made his wife throw her arms around him joyfully.

He told her he had finally decided to take a job that

would bring in a regular salary. The pay for his new post in the Customs House in New York City was not very generous, but with the money they had inherited from Judge Cady it would now become possible for them all to move away from Seneca Falls.

So Neil could enter Columbia College. And Kit and Gat could prepare for the same institution. At least until they finished their higher education, they would surely delay any further thought of donning uniforms.

No matter that moving their large family was almost as complicated as moving a whole army; Mrs. Stanton hesitated not an instant. That very evening she wrote begging Susan to come help with the packing. Then while Henry Stanton went off to rent a house in the city, box after box was dragged down from the attic or up from the cellar. As soon as Susan B. arrived, she gave all the children a big hug—and then immediately gave each of them a job. Even Maggie and Hattie were put in charge of carrying books to load into boxes.

Meanwhile their mother sat in the midst of all this activity, writing a new speech.

For nothing could put woman's rights completely out of her mind. Despite family problems and the threat of war, Mrs. Stanton had kept in close touch with the situation in Albany. Some years earlier, a small victory had been achieved, and yet it was not a victory for which she could claim any credit. Owing largely to the efforts of a few rich men whose daughters had married unwisely, the legislature had passed a new law giving married women some control over the money they inherited from their own families. So dishonest sons-in-law were no longer able to waste their wives' fortunes.

However, even though any wider reform was considered quite unnecessary by some lawmakers, a growing number seemed to feel more of an interest in the whole subject of woman's rights. Thus for the second time Mrs. Stanton prepared to address the New York State Legislature.

This time her speech was taken more seriously. After she finished talking, a new law was introduced—and it passed. By its terms, married women living in the Empire State could own property of various sorts. They would now have a legal right to keep any wages they earned themselves. They could appear in court, and their own children could not legally be taken away from them.

They still could not vote. Nevertheless, Mrs. Stanton felt a tremendous sense of triumph. While hundreds of other women had worked hard toward the same end, she was proud of her own part in bringing about the victory.

But before she could plan her next steps, the dreaded news came from South Carolina:

CONFLICT AT CHARLESTON
Hostilities have been begun by the
forces of the Confederate States . . .

Now a terrible civil war had started.

8

 "THE REVOLUTION"

DURING THE FIRST YEARS OF THE WAR, MRS. STANTON was unavoidably taken up with family matters. But once she had all her children settled in their schools, and as soon as she learned how to manage her tall and narrow city house, she began casting about for some useful way of occupying herself.

While she was still learning to cope with having four flights of stairs to climb from her front door up to the boys' bedrooms—plus another flight down to her kitchen in the basement—she suffered a severe disappointment. Without even giving her a chance to rush to Albany, the legislature changed the new woman's rights law, removing several of its most important sections.

What cowards these men were! Mrs. Stanton complained bitterly to Susan that she felt as if she had been stabbed in the back!

Yet Mrs. Stanton really understood that moving ahead on the reform closest to her heart would have to wait until the terrible war ended. The pro-slavery forces had to be beaten before further progress could be made on any other front. Would it not be possible, though, to find some way to help the Union cause, and at the same time to help the cause of women?

Of course! So with a great flurry of letter writing, Mrs. Stanton set about organizing the Women's National Loyal League. As always, Susan took on the task of carrying out her friend's plans. She attended to countless details like raising money and renting an office. Early in 1863, the new group held its first meeting.

Even those newspapers that liked to scoff at "hen conventions" were impressed when hundreds of respectable-looking ladies crowded into the Cooper Institute, one of New York City's larger halls. By now, dozens of women from various parts of the country had emerged as leaders in the equal rights movement, and most of them listened approvingly as Mrs. Stanton stated her views about what the league's basic policy should be.

"There never can be a true peace in this Republic," she said, "until the civil and political rights of all citizens of African descent *and of all women* are practically established." Thus she proposed that the league should work toward both of these objectives.

As soon as Mrs. Stanton finished speaking, Mrs. Angelina Weld stood up. Back in the 1830's, before marrying an abolitionist, Miss Angelina Grimké of South Carolina had shocked many people all over the country. The daughter of a rich slaveowner, she had dared to give a series of lectures telling the evils she had seen with her own eyes on her family's plantation. Now, thirty years later, she said, "I rejoice that Mrs. Stanton's resolution should combine us with the Negro. Until he gets his rights, we shall never have ours."

The next speaker was Mrs. Ernestine Rose, who had been born in Poland but had mastered English to the extent that she was becoming famous as a female orator. "It is a painful fact," she said, "that woman under the law has been in the same category with the slave."

Although not disputing this point, some of the other women at the meeting raised a problem. Would it not antagonize many people who opposed slavery, but still felt unconcerned about the woman question, if the two issues were linked together by the new league?

That was a risk they must take take, Miss Anthony said crisply. And her opinion prevailed. When the debate ended, the group voted in favor of adopting the two goals, and then it also elected a president. Her name was Elizabeth Cady Stanton.

Mrs. Stanton was delighted by her new title, and she immediately showed she meant to set a fine example for all future female officeholders. Within a few weeks she had her league hard at work on the most ambitious project any women's group had ever undertaken.

For President Lincoln was moving much too slowly to suit her. After two years of hesitating, he had finally come out with an Emancipation Proclamation. That document was a step in the right direction, she had to admit, but only a timid step because it granted freedom just to certain categories of slaves. What the nation really needed—and her husband had given her this idea

—was an amendment to the United States Constitution guaranteeing the full rights of citizenship to every black person everywhere under the American flag.

However, it struck Mrs. Stanton all by herself that her women could make Congress consider passing such an amendment. If they circulated petitions in every free state, they might well gather thousands and thousands of signatures. Indeed, she saw no reason not to aim for a nice, round number. For instance, one million.

Such a mass effort had never before been attempted, but Mrs. Stanton cheerfully brushed aside suggestions that her goal was impossible. And one man did share her optimism. He was Senator Charles Sumner of Massachusetts, the leader of the radical wing of the Republican party. "Send me the petitions as fast as you receive them," he wrote. "They give me opportunities for speech."

Certainly! Mrs. Stanton could scarcely contain her high spirits as she talked to Susan about the petition drive. For if they did Senator Sumner the great favor of providing him with ammunition in his fight to win this amendment, surely he would owe the women of America a huge debt. And Lizzie Stanton knew exactly how she wanted the debt to be paid. The same amendment to the Constitution that gave black citizens equal rights would also give full citizenship to the nation's females!

But how could they be sure Senator Sumner would see the matter in the same light as they did? Susan frowned as she asked this, for she could not quite share her friend's enthusiasm. Mrs. Stanton airily dismissed Susan's worries, though. The whole art of politics was based on doing favors, she assured her. So if the women did Senator Sumner a favor, he was bound to do them one in return.

Then, Mrs. Stanton said triumphantly, in only a few years they would be celebrating total victory by this wonderful shortcut. They would not even have to bother with state legislatures any more. Why, they might even be able to vote for the next President!

Being so positive that she was on the right track at last, Mrs. Stanton flung every ounce of her energy into her new campaign. As usual, she took charge of the grand strategy while Susan did the down-to-earth job of getting the petitions printed and thousands of volunteers enlisted. Once again, their teamwork proved effective. By the end of that summer they had 300,000 names to send to Washington.

And sack after sack of signed petitions kept arriving at Miss Anthony's cubbyhole of an office near the City Hall. They came from Maine and even from Texas—so many bags that the individual names could no longer be counted. By the spring of 1864, the Senate was ready to discuss Mr. Sumner's amendment.

However, neither Mr. Sumner nor any other senator was ready to sponsor a single sentence about woman's rights. "It's the Negro's hour," they kept saying. "If you women will wait a bit, your turn will come."

At first Mrs. Stanton accepted these words without feeling too discouraged. She had absolutely convinced herself, as she had tried to convince Susan, that victory was just around the corner. Thus she could not even imagine any other outcome.

However, after the Thirteenth and then the Fourteenth and then the Fifteenth amendments to the Constitution were all adopted, Mrs. Stanton could no longer hide the truth from herself. She had been betrayed!

For these three amendments made black men full citizens, at least in the legal sense. But not a single new right was granted to any woman, white or black.

Senator Sumner and his friends had been more than willing to accept the help of America's women. Yet these men were not willing to give the women their just reward. Never again, Lizzie Stanton fumed, would she trust in the honor of any political figure.

What made matters still worse, as far as Mrs. Stanton was concerned, was that so many people she had thought of as firm friends deserted her. She was not too surprised when Wendell Phillips shrugged off the women's claims by murmuring, "It's the Negro's hour, you know." For she well remembered how he had taken the same sort of cowardly escape back in London in 1840. However, now even William Lloyd Garrison would not protest this new injustice to women. Nor did Horace Greeley.

Worst of all, though, some women who had given much of their lives to the cause—women like Lucy Stone who had been bravely fighting for equality as long as Lizzie Stanton herself—even some of these women mildly said that the ending of Negro slavery was victory enough for the time being.

Not that Mrs. Stanton felt any less happy than Lucy Stone did when their black friends won freedom. She felt just as joyful, too, when the Union side won the war. Although she had often fretted about Mr. Lincoln's indecisiveness, she also mourned him sincerely when he was shot down.

But the woman's cause was still uppermost in Mrs. Stanton's mind, and she could not forgive Mr. Sumner or his friends. Her feelings on this subject were so strong that she became thoroughly depressed for the first time in her life—until Kansas raised her hopes.

In 1867, that young state decided to hold the nation's first election contest on the issue of woman suffrage.

Should the women of Kansas be allowed to vote? This question was going to be put to the men of Kansas in the coming November, and Mrs. Stanton danced a little jig when she heard the great news. Then instantly she began making plans. All of the best speakers for the cause must hurry out to crisscross the state, holding meetings in even the smallest settlements.

Within a few weeks, she had firm promises from practically everybody she approached. Lucy Stone would go. Fred Douglass, who might have a wide appeal because abolitionist sentiment had been particularly strong out there, said he was willing. "If you can forgive me for being a Negro," he wrote to Mrs. Stanton, "I cannot do less than forgive you for being a woman." Susan, of course, would also make the trip.

And so would Lizzie Stanton. Now her oldest boys were finishing law school, and even her youngest was old enough to be left with relatives for several months. Mrs. Stanton not only leaped at her first chance to see the West, but now, at the age of fifty-two, she announced that the time had come for the whole family to become pioneers.

The East was finished, she said scornfully. Why, just consider the shameful way the woman's movement was being ignored by the established powers of the eastern coast! During her speaking tour, she told her husband, she would make a point of looking for a likely site for them to start a new life in the pure air of the West.

Henry Stanton's mustache had turned completely gray by this time. Having resumed his newspaper work, he was now a regular editorial writer for Mr. Greeley's highly regarded *New York Tribune*. He felt quite satisfied with living and working in the nation's biggest city. However, after twenty-seven years of being married to the former Lizzie Cady, he knew better than to argue with her. He merely nodded and said her idea might possibly be a good one. Privately, his feeling was that if she did not give up this ridiculous notion, there would still be plenty of time for letting her hear his true opinion.

Mrs. Stanton had by no means changed her mind when she boarded a train with Susan late in August. Even after riding 1500 miles, stifling in a closed railway coach most of the way or else choking from the engine's soot if a window was opened, she remained convinced. On arriving at Topeka, she dashed off a letter to her husband:

> This is the country for us to move to. The Governor has a handsome house. We could build one for $3,000.
>
> Ponies are cheap here, so that all the children could ride and breathe and learn to do big things. . . .
>
> You, too, would feel like a new being here. You could be a leader as there is not a man in the state that can make a really good speech.

But soon enough her rosy first impressions began fading. In order to reach the largest possible number of voters, it seemed best for her and Susan to separate. Since Mrs. Stanton had become rather plump during recent years and her hair had turned pure white, a former governor who sympathized with her cause offered to travel with her. However, she quickly lost any sense of being treated as a helpless old lady.

Because most of the state had not yet attracted the notice of railroad builders, Mr. Robinson provided a low-slung carriage drawn by two horses for their journey. Mrs. Stanton received a hint of what lay in store for them when he stowed assorted refreshments under the seat. Along with a bushel of apples, a bag of crackers, and a pail of water for the horses, he somehow made room for their valises and also a large box of leaflets about why women should be allowed to vote.

Then with a sharp snap of his whip, they drove out of Topeka.

Mrs. Stanton was wearing her customary black dress and neat white collar and cuffs. Her eyes alertly scanned the rolling expanse of tall grass on either side of the narrow dirt road. At last, she thought, here was the unspoiled prairie she had so longed to see.

Perhaps that clump of trees on the far horizon was at this very moment sheltering a wagon train of pioneers, stopping to enjoy a picnic lunch in the shade. How brave these westbound families were! Could even Sir Walter Scott's heroes match the romance of the simple life in Kansas?

During the next several weeks, Mrs. Stanton learned a great deal. She learned about dried herring and greasy stew, and about bedbugs and fleas. Besides enduring all manner of discomforts in eating and sleeping —just as the pioneers did, as she soon discovered—she also learned how it felt to be lost in the wilderness.

Often the approach of darkness would find them miles from any sign of human habitation. Then Governor Robinson would hand her the reins and step down to lead the way as best he could on foot. He took off his coat, so she would be able to keep her eyes on the white of his shirt sleeves. Feeling all but paralyzed by her fear that the horses would stumble going down a hill or sink into the mud when they had to ford a stream, she somehow managed to seem calm and cool through every adventure. Indeed, the governor frequently complimented her on her courage.

Ha! Mrs. Stanton wondered what he would say if she admitted that she was too frightened to cry out.

Yet she would not have missed this experience for anything. Despite all the hardships, she felt more fully alive than she had in years. It was satisfying beyond belief to know she was facing real perils, and she was not disgracing her sex.

In fact, she was helping women everywhere, of that she was certain. During the two hard months she spent in Kansas, she never ceased spreading the message that wives who fully shared the constant dangers of pioneering well deserved to share the rights of citizenship too.

Wherever a dozen voters could be assembled, Mrs. Stanton stopped to speak up for her cause. She spoke in log cabins and unfinished schoolhouses; in churches, barns, and even in the open air. One evening she addressed people who had gathered from twenty miles around in a large field lighted only by the glow of a few lanterns.

Yet Mrs. Stanton met an enemy in Kansas she had never met before. Sentiment in favor of giving women equal rights ran strong here, as was clearly shown by the fact that this was the first state even to consider granting women the basic right of voting. However, another force had also entered into the contest.

What would women do with the vote if they were allowed to cast ballots?

Why, they would undoubtedly raise the general level of election campaigns, Mrs. Stanton said. For women would surely support the best candidates, and they would also support laws improving their communities.

"But you can bet the ladies will push through a law

you won't like." That was the reply some men kept giving to the same question.

For the temperance movement was winning many friends among the women of Kansas. In all of the larger communities, there were active groups working to discourage the sale of beer and whisky. Not only tavernkeepers, but also many men who enjoyed taking a drink or two became seriously concerned about the woman suffrage issue.

Why take a chance that the ladies might be able to pass a law banning all alcoholic beverages?

When Mrs. Stanton learned that this was what many men were saying, she shook her head disgustedly. No doubt the brewers and the tavern owners of the state were paying out money to spread this rumor. Yet the sensible men of Kansas must surely realize that women alone could not force the passage of such a law.

However, Mrs. Stanton underestimated the strength of this new enemy, and of the traditional idea that woman's place was in the home. When the votes were counted in November, woman suffrage was approved by only about 9,000 men. Nearly 21,000 others voted against it.

Under ordinary circumstances, Mrs. Stanton might have been crushed by the defeat. The verdict was not even close, despite all the effort she and the rest of the pro-suffrage speakers had put into this campaign. Nevertheless, her spirits had never been higher—for she was about to start *The Revolution*.

•9•

ON THE ROAD

HER *Revolution* HAPPENED ONCE A WEEK. MRS. STAN-
ton had been dreaming for many years about having a
newspaper of her own. At last, in Kansas, she found
someone willing to help her make her dream come true.

He was a man named George Francis Train, and he
was one of the oddest characters imaginable. Having
made a great deal of money in one bold venture after
another, having to do with clipper ships and railroad
lines, he could afford to indulge his taste for unusual
clothing. Among his favorite trimmings were brass but-
tons, patent leather boots, and lavender kid gloves. He
could also afford to spend freely on causes that appealed to him.

How Mr. Train first became interested in woman
suffrage Mrs. Stanton never learned. But any friend of
this cause was bound to strike her as a person of sound
judgment. When she saw a poster advertising one of
his Kansas meetings, she made a point of being in the
audience.

His platform manner astonished her no less than it did the rest of his hearers. Prancing back and forth across a stage, he shook his fist dramatically. Any man who refused to vote in favor of the ladies, he shouted, was positively insulting his mother, his sisters, his wife, and his daughters.

Roars of laughter greeted Mr. Train's every remark. But while Mrs. Stanton could see that he made a comical figure, she refused to doubt his good sense. Thus when he offered to give her the money to start her own newspaper in New York City, she gratefully accepted his help.

The only condition he set was that some of his other pet ideas about politics and business were to be backed in the paper's columns. A well-known writer, Parker Pillsbury, agreed to do this part of the editing task. Again Susan Anthony would see to such details as hiring a printer and enlisting subscribers. Otherwise Mrs. Stanton would be entirely on her own, right from the first step of giving the new weekly its name.

Instead of turning more conservative as she grew older, she gave every sign of becoming increasingly radical. For she hesitated not an instant about choosing to call her newspaper *The Revolution*. Even Susan Anthony protested this might frighten away many readers, and also make it harder to secure articles from authors like Harriet Beecher Stowe. For Mrs. Stowe had already said she would be happy to contribute to a woman's journal if its title were less disturbing.

"As to changing the name of *The Revolution*," Mrs. Stanton wrote to Miss Anthony, "I should consider it a great mistake. There could not be a better name. The establishing of woman on her rightful throne is the greatest revolution the world has ever known or ever will know. To bring it about is no child's play. You and I have not forgotten the conflict of the last twenty years —the ridicule, persecution, denunciation.

"A journal called *The Rosebud* might answer for those who come with white gloves and perfume. But for us there is no name like *The Revolution*."

In her first issue, which appeared on January 8, 1868, Mrs. Stanton proved that she really did mean to shake up public opinion as much as she possibly could. Her slogan, she announced, was: "Down with politicians; up with the people!" Any topic of interest to womankind would be openly discussed in her pages, she promised.

Then she kept her word by printing regular articles on such daring subjects as the need for major reforms of the divorce laws. Even religion was not too sacred for her to write sarcastically about the anti-female bias of many church leaders. She also adopted a startling new policy concerning advertising. She refused to publish an ad unless the product being described measured up to her own high standards.

As long as she was able to keep putting out a new issue of *The Revolution* every week, Mrs. Stanton had the time of her life. The office Susan had rented was

The Revolution,
Devoted to the discussion of
SUFFRAGE,
The only means by which
EQUAL RIGHTS
can be secured to
WOMAN
in the STATE, the CHURCH, the HOME and the
World of WORK.
AN AMERICAN MONETARY SYSTEM—
Greenbacks for money, as well for Bondholders and
Capitalists, as for the Working Classes.

ELIZABETH CADY STANTON,
PARKER PILLSBURY,
Editors.

Terms—Two Dollars a year in advance. Five
names ($10) entitle the sender to one copy free.
New York City subscribers, $2.50.
All Communications should be addressed to the
Proprietor, SUSAN B. ANTHONY,
Revolution Office,
No. 49 East 23d St., (Woman's Bureau,)
New York.

To be had of the American News Co. and the
New York News Co., New York; the Western News
Co., Chicago, and the St. Louis Book and News Co.,
St. Louis.

The Revolution,

No. 49 East 23d St., (Woman's Bureau.)

New York, Sept 2nd 1869.

Dear Mr Greely,

I will be happy to meet you at the Bureau Friday morning as you suggest

sincerely yours

Elizabeth Cady Stanton

A note Mrs. Stanton dashed off to Horace Greeley from her
office at *The Revolution*

Manuscript Division, The New York Public Library,
Astor, Lenox and Tilden Foundations

no ordinary, sloppy print shop littered with piles of dusty papers. A neat carpet covered the floor, and not a speck of dust was allowed to settle on any surface. In a small inner sanctum, Mrs. Stanton sat at her desk looking completely happy while she covered page after page with her bold, slanting handwriting. If only Mr. Train had been more reliable, she might contentedly have spent the rest of her days there.

Besides being an able writer, she also showed a rare talent for coping with the mechanical problems of creating a newspaper. To make sure that her journal would be easy to read, she used the best-quality ink and avoided crowding her pages with a jumble of tiny lines of type, as so many other editors did. Despite *The Revolution's* brash tone, it attracted favorable comment from an increasing number of readers, and from some competitors too. For instance, the *Cincinnati Enquirer* noted, "Mrs. Elizabeth Cady Stanton's *Revolution* grows with each additional number more spicy, readable and revolutionary. It hits right and left, from the shoulder and overhand at everybody and thing . . ."

However, Mr. Train sadly disappointed Mrs. Stanton, after all. Some new scheme made him rush off to England, where his actions became so peculiar that he was put in a lunatic asylum. Although Susan Anthony tried desperately to keep paying *The Revolution's* bills, the paper was not earning enough money and, before three years had passed, the final issue appeared.

By then it had already caused more trouble than even

Mrs. Stanton relished. A good many supporters of woman's rights were distressed by having someone like Mr. Train welcomed into their ranks. Any person who accepted help from such a quarter was showing very poor judgment, they kept saying. Still Lizzie Stanton stubbornly insisted she had done quite right in letting Mr. Train contribute as much as he had. Writing to one of her old friends, she assured her, "Time will show that Miss Anthony and I are neither idiots nor lunatics."

Yet this did not end the matter. In 1869, the first national convention of the woman's rights movement assembled in Washington, D.C. At the age of seventy-six, Lucretia Mott left her country fireside near Philadelphia to preside over the opening session. Looking more saintly than ever, the frail old lady inspired all those present to rise in warm tribute. One journalist reporting on the meeting wrote that Mrs. Mott represented the soul of the feminist movement, while Mrs. Stanton was its mind and Miss Anthony its main force of energy.

But as the sessions continued, it became clear that some of the delegates no longer trusted either Mrs. Stanton or Miss Anthony. By their willingness to join forces with Mr. Train, these two leaders had lost the confidence of many of their followers. In addition, *The Revolution* itself upset the same women. They finally got so angry at the way Mrs. Stanton spoke up during the course of the meeting that they marched out to form their own separate organization.

A cartoon of Mrs. Stanton poking fun at her for daring to argue
with leading clergymen about woman's rights

So from 1869 onward, the equal rights movement was divided into two parts. The split thoroughly confused most people because both groups picked similar names. The more conservative—calling itself the American Woman Suffrage Association—was led by Lucy Stone, and it probably spoke for a larger number of the women who took any active interest in the whole question. However, the more radical—the National Woman Suffrage Association, led by Mrs. Stanton and Miss Anthony—undoubtedly spoke louder.

Beyond the general difference of outlook that marked the two groups, a specific policy kept them apart. Lucy Stone's supporters took the view that winning new rights could best be accomplished gradually, by convincing the members of the various state legislatures about the justice of the woman's cause. Then when one state after another changed its laws, the women of the whole country would at last be full citizens. It was not realistic to expect such a great change to occur overnight, Lucy Stone said mildly. Even if no woman now alive ever cast a ballot, they should all take heart from the fact that their granddaughters would doubtless be voters.

Should they really? Mrs. Stanton turned sarcastic when she had to listen to nonsense of this sort. In her eyes, it was perfectly clear that America's women must follow a different strategy to achieve their rightful goals. Having already spent so much of her strength making vain appeals to state legislatures, she had little faith in these bodies. The events of the past few years

had taught her a lesson. She tho
route to the voting booth was by way
Just as slavery had finally been ended b.
Constitution, so women would finally wi.
in the same manner.

Thus she and Miss Anthony held their gi
nual meetings in the nation's capital. They pu their
main hope on getting support in Congress for a six-
teenth amendment, which would grant the women of
every state the basic right to vote.

At the same time, Mrs. Stanton started a new program of her own. She still felt that the West offered the
most promising field for anyone interested in progress,
although she had given up her notion of permanently
settling there. Instead she adopted a plan to help her
cause, and also to satisfy several personal goals.

With the failure of *The Revolution*, she needed some
new outlet for her urge to express herself. She had a
particular reason, too, for wanting to earn as much
money as she possibly could. Her husband's income,
together with the sum that remained from her own
inheritance, had proved sufficient to send their four
oldest boys through college. But now her daughters,
Maggie and Hattie, were arriving at an age where they
could think of seeking higher education, and now there
were several colleges that were accepting female students. While Henry Stanton was willing to have his
girls enter one of these institutions, he did not see how
he could afford the extra expense.

So his wife calmly told him she would provide the

essary funds. And she could not help feeling rather
pleased by the fact that a leading lecture agency
snapped at the chance to add her name to its list of
speakers. She also liked the idea of seeing as much as
she could of the whole country. Deep inside her, she
felt still another sense of release. After spending long
years all but chained to her household up in Seneca
Falls while her husband enjoyed complete freedom, she
thought he deserved a taste of his own medicine. Now
she would go on the road and let him stay put for a
change.

Not that supervising their city household presented
many problems these days. Even young Robbie was
almost grown, and no longer needed constant watching
to be kept from tossing a ball too widely and breaking
some neighbor's window. Between the girls and dear old
Mrs. Willard, every type of domestic chore could easily
be accomplished. Nor could New York City be com-
pared to Seneca Falls.

In at least one respect, though, the new arrangement
Mrs. Stanton decided on after *The Revolution* failed
served the same purpose her husband's travels had
served many years earlier. It kept these two very strong
personalities from clashing continuously. They had been
married for more than a quarter of a century, and they
remained extremely fond of each other. Nevertheless,
neither of them could help coming out with definite
opinions on every kind of question. If they went their
own separate ways during a good part of the year, then

Greatly in demand as a speaker, Mrs. Stanton carried her message about woman's rights from Maine to California

the time they did spend together was bound to be much happier.

So Mrs. Stanton boarded a train soon after her newspaper stopped appearing. From October to June, just as regularly as the autumn followed the summer, she

..t out to spread her message about woman's rights on platforms all the way from Maine to California. Wherever she spoke, she made new friends for her cause and she also earned at least one hundred dollars. By the end of each trip she had a handsome profit, beyond all her expenses, totaling several thousand dollars. In addition, she had a matchless collection of adventures to relate.

Mrs. Stanton was fifty-five years old when she began lecturing practically every evening in a different town. Her fondness for thick cream in her coffee and large helpings of apple pie had kept adding to her weight, but she still had the fresh, rosy complexion of her girlhood. Nor had she lost the young Lizzie Cady's high spirits.

Once she was marooned in an Iowa town when the conductor of the train she had been riding announced that the road ahead was blocked by snowdrifts. Undaunted, Mrs. Stanton sought out the landlord of the local inn. "I must be in Maquoketa at eight o'clock tonight," she told him. "Do you have a sleigh and a skillful driver?"

"Why, yes," he said, "but you could not stand a six-hour drive in this piercing wind."

At that, she informed him that she had grown up in snow country herself, where the temperature often went to twenty degrees below zero. She most certainly could stand the trip if she could find the proper equipment. Thus, wrapped in a fur cloak and with a buffalo robe on her lap, a hot oak plank for her feet, and a veil over her face and head to give extra protection from the wind, off she went.

Since not a train in the area was running, Mrs. Stanton surprised the committee that had planned her meeting by appearing right on time. But she surprised one of her fellow lecturers even more. He was a Civil War general who had taken part in many battles, and she met him when she arrived back in Chicago. He was waiting there until the roads were cleared, he said, and he had already missed several of his speaking engagements.

"I seem to remember," Mrs. Stanton remarked, "that you marched with Sherman to the sea. And yet this blizzard has stopped you!"

The general admitted it.

"I suppose," said Mrs. Stanton, "that you still consider women are the weaker sex."

Neither snow nor floods kept her from following the schedule her tour manager had arranged for her. Neither leaking roofs nor crying babies in the audience kept her from standing up on the platform with a cheerful smile. Somehow her white collar and cuffs always looked newly laundered, and even when her baggage got lost she managed to borrow suitable attire despite the fact that she was becoming rather wider than the general run of womankind.

Food. That was her worst problem during her traveling. By dint of constant practice, she taught herself to sleep almost anywhere, even curled up on the hard wood bench of a depot while she was waiting for a train. But the watery tea and leaden bread that passed for refreshment at many stops along the road depressed her sadly. When she did have the good fortune to be offered some decent nourishment at the home of someone in one of her audiences, she could not help taking full advantage of her opportunity. As a result, no matter that she missed many a meal, still she more than amply made up for these losses by taking an extra piece of pie at her next stop—and so even though she was always on the go, her girth kept steadily increasing.

But her zest for new experiences stayed as strong as ever. At odd moments along her way she wrote to various members of her family, and in spite of the many horrible mishaps she had to report she still left no doubt that she was really enjoying herself. In the spring of 1872 her sister Kate received this letter from Nebraska:

Monday I rode in an open wagon 30 miles across the prairies, spoke that evening and the next morning, and in the afternoon rode the same distance back again. Then I took the railroad to Hastings, where I arrived at 11 p.m., and as there was an exciting murder trial on, I could not get a place to sleep. So, with my clothes all on, I lay on a broken-down old lounge, sleeping on the points of some springs and bumps until one side of my body was partially paralyzed, and then getting up and walking for awhile before trying the other side. I thought the night would never end. The next morning, after a meagre breakfast, I was packed into a long omnibus filled with men, women, children, babies, bags, and bundles, with a conceited boy of sixteen in charge of the precious cargo, who whipped the horses around the corners as if the devil was after him. I expected every moment that we would be upset and my expectations were realized. Dashing up to the depot and wishing to show off before a crowd of men and boys, all in town to attend the trial, we were overturned, on my side, the blow coming full force on the back of my head. Several of the passengers were badly hurt and all emerged from the wreck with torn garments and disheveled locks. But strange to say, I came out of the mess without a scratch or bruise that I can see, though my head and back have ached constantly. Since then I have spoken every night, traveling on the train during the day. Everybody regards me with wonder for my endurance and cheerfulness, and I must say that, comparing myself to most women, I have come to the conclusion that I was well born, and that my parents put me together with unusual wisdom and discretion; for all of which I am devoutly thankful. I enjoy life under the most adverse circumstances.

Then, after her daughter Maggie entered Vassar College, Mrs. Stanton snatched a few minutes out in Utah to answer a letter that had just been forwarded to her. "You ask if it is not lonely traveling as I do," she wrote. "It is indeed, and I should have enjoyed above all things having Hattie [who was still at home] here with me." Then she went on to explain:

But you see, dearest, that would double my expenses, and I am so desirous of making money for the household, I must practice economy in some direction. And above all considerations of loneliness and fatigue, I feel as if I am doing an immense amount of good in rousing women to thought and inspiring them with new hope and self respect, that I am making the path smoother for you and Hattie and all the other dear girls.

Along her travels, Mrs. Stanton also did all she could —and that was no small amount—to improve the lot of her fellow passengers, particularly little babies. The sound of an infant crying always roused her to action. On entering a railroad car one morning, she was horrified to discover some young parents alternately shaking and slapping their wailing baby. "If you don't stop it," the father finally shouted, "I'll throw you out of the window!"

That was too much for Mrs. Stanton to bear in silence. "Let me take your child and see if I can find out what ails it," she suggested.

"Nothing ails it," the father said bitterly. "Nothing but bad temper."

Still, the child readily came onto Mrs. Stanton's broad lap while she felt around to see if its clothes pinched anywhere or a pin was pricking it. Then she took off the baby's hat and cloak to find out if any strings were choking it. On past occasions, she had comforted numerous infants by this sort of investigation. Now Mrs. Stanton was forced to look further for the source of the trouble. She glanced at the baby's feet, then finally nodded in triumph.

The child's boots were at least a full size too small! Taking them off, she found prints of the tight laces clearly traced on the tender young flesh. So she sat rubbing the little feet till the poor baby felt better and fell asleep.

"You are young people, I see," Mrs. Stanton said then to the parents. "This is probably your first child. You don't intend to be cruel, I know, but if you had thrown those boots out of the window when you threatened to throw the child, it would have been wiser."

The mother admitted she had thought the boots must be too small because it had been so hard to get them on, but the child's only other pair was too shabby for wearing on a journey.

Mrs. Stanton shook her head solemnly. "Let me give you one rule," she said. "When your child cries, remember it is telling you as well as it can that something hurts it, either outside or in, and do not rest until you can find out what it is. Neither spanking, shaking, nor scolding can relieve the pain."

More often, though, the main discomfort afflicting the traveling public, young and old, was a simple lack of fresh air. So every time Mrs. Stanton boarded a train, she immediately searched for some way of improving the ventilation. One midnight when she entered a car nearly as stuffy as the Black Hole of Calcutta, she briskly moved among the sleeping passengers till she discovered the location of the heating stove. She shut the stove, opened an air vent in the ceiling with a poker, and then for good measure took a stick of wood to prop the car's door ajar. As a refreshing blast of cool night air blew in, a sleeping man stirred fitfully. "We must be going north," he muttered.

For twelve years Mrs. Stanton kept riding back and forth across the country, until even she decided she was too old for living out of a suitcase and lecturing nearly every evening. Toward the end of this period, Henry Stanton had startled his wife by indicating that he was almost ready to retire. Though he was well past seventy, he still stood as tall as he had long ago when they first met. His hair was gray now, and hers was white, yet they both felt younger than they really were. Nevertheless, they agreed around the time of their fortieth wedding anniversary, in 1880, to build a cozy little house across the Hudson River from New York City. Here in the peace of rural New Jersey they planned to spend their remaining days.

·10·

GOOD OLD LIZZIE!

EVERYTHING CONSIDERED, MRS. STANTON DID RATHER
well at keeping her resolve to take life easier when she
stopped lecturing. She spent the better part of the next
several years without ranging very far from her New
Jersey retreat—except, of course, to attend the annual
meetings of the National Woman Suffrage Association
in Washington, and to testify before committees of lawmakers, and to dash off for visits with old friends all
over the East.

Not that she took up knitting or some similar pastime
while she stayed home in Tenafly. On the contrary, she
worked more steadily than she ever had, even in her
younger days. During the preceding four decades she
had accumulated a vast collection of letters, clippings,
and speeches about the woman question, and Susan
Anthony also had stacks of boxes filled with reports on
the same subject. Mrs. Stanton fully realized that unless
something were done, and done fairly soon, to sift

through all this yellowing paper, a priceless gold mine would be lost. For when the United States did grant equal rights to its female citizens, as she was still positive would happen, then how could the true story of this great reform be written if the records telling its early chapters had already disappeared?

Actually, the arrival of her own sixty-fifth birthday in 1880 had first raised the question in her mind. It was the very day that dear Lucretia Mott died at the age of eighty-seven, and with her departure Mrs. Stanton could not help thinking what a shame it would be if such a noble example to her sex should ever be forgotten. Surely those who remembered Mrs. Mott owed her the duty of seeing that her words and deeds were preserved to inspire future generations.

So Mrs. Stanton started to keep a diary that day, and she put down some of her fondest memories of her old friend. Yet she soon decided that merely jotting a few recollections would not accomplish what she wanted. Despite being a bit short of breath after she had to climb a flight of stairs, she still felt ready for a new adventure every morning. One fine morning she got the notion of writing a detailed history of the whole woman's movement.

That was why she lured Susan into coming over to live temporarily in Tenafly. Then, together, they started poring through mounds of old documents and newspapers. Laughing, talking, and squabbling all day long, they sat at a round table beside a sunny window, thoroughly absorbed by the task they had set themselves. For the better part of four years they kept reading and writing. The fruit of this labor was four thick volumes, each containing well over a thousand printed pages.

After their *History of Woman Suffrage* was sent to libraries in every part of the country, Mrs. Stanton did not say that her outlook had changed. Hardly anyone but Susan Anthony suspected it, and Miss Anthony preferred pretending there had been no change.

Lizzie Stanton herself knew the truth, though. Almost as if she had taken a heavy weight that she had been carrying for most of her life and placed it on a shelf along with those huge books she and Susan had just produced, she felt like a new person.

The woman's movement still interested her; she could not even imagine that the day would ever come when a case of unfairness toward a female would fail to stir her deeply. In this world or the next, she cheerfully told Susan, she would always keep her own special brand of thunderbolt handy for smiting all enemies of their sex.

Nevertheless, as Mrs. Stanton approached her seventieth birthday, she made it more and more clear that other interests were now taking a larger share of her remaining energy. Although her sons had been in no hurry to marry, possibly following the example of their own parents, there were several weddings at Tenafly during the 1880's. These increases in the size of her family delighted Mrs. Stanton.

When her fourth son, Theodore, who had spent several years studying in Europe, arrived home with a French bride, she felt a bit sad about having missed their wedding ceremony. But as soon as she met Theo's new wife, she could not help approving of his choice.

Furthermore, Theodore's marriage proved to be the most important factor in setting a pleasant new pattern for his mother's old age. Because of Marguerite's family ties, and because Theo wanted to write about European politics, the young couple settled in Paris. Despite her own advancing years, Mrs. Stanton had not lost her zest for traveling. Thus she began making a trip to France almost every summer, particularly after she had the added incentive of going to see the French grand-daughter named Lisette in her honor.

Then little Lisette, at least indirectly, opened even wider possibilities. One summer Mrs. Stanton brought her own daughter, Hattie, abroad, supposedly to practice speaking French but really to meet this charming child. During the same visit, Hattie made another acquaintance. A young Englishman who already had several female relatives interested in woman's rights invited Miss Stanton and her mother to stay with his family outside of London before sailing back across the Atlantic.

As a result, Mrs. Stanton had one more wedding to enjoy the following year. Then after Hattie became Mrs. Blatch of Basingstoke, England, Mrs. Stanton found good reason for boarding a steamer earlier in the season and remaining abroad longer on each trip.

Three generations—Elizabeth Cady Stanton with her daughter Harriot Blatch and her English granddaughter

The New York Public Library

It was at Basingstoke, where she was holding a tiny English granddaughter on her lap, that Mrs. Stanton received a cable from America in 1887. This gave her the sad news she told herself she should have been more prepared to receive. Six months before his eighty-second birthday, her husband, who had seemed as sturdy as ever when she had last seen him, had suddenly suffered a heart attack and died.

Although Mrs. Stanton had never made a habit of trying to avoid facing unpleasant facts, she realized now that Henry had become an old man without her noticing it. It distressed her that she had left him on his own so often during recent years. Yet he had been busy writing a book, he had friends who kept him in good spirits, and he had not appeared to be disturbed by her frequent absences. Instead of blaming herself, she mused, perhaps she ought to take comfort from reflecting that he had enjoyed a reasonably long life. And in their own way they had been very happy together.

Mrs. Stanton also had the consolation of being firmly convinced that there was some form of life after death. While no organized religion appealed to her, she had over the years worked out her own private system of religious belief. That partly explained her calm attitude about growing old herself.

On her next birthday, she was going to be seventy-two but she refused to feel any regret for the passing years. In her diary, she frequently wrote about the way she kept discovering new pleasures. "How I do rejoice in the lights and shadows of the sunset hour," she noted one evening. She wrote, too, of "the rich autumnal colors, the rustling leaves, the gentle breezes whispering to them as they fall."

Indeed, her state of mind was so peaceful that she was invited many times during these years to speak at meetings of one group or another on this very subject, "The Pleasures of Old Age." Until the prospect of mingling with crowds of strangers began to seem too tiring, she gladly gave this speech on many occasions.

Of course, she also spoke on her favorite subject of woman suffrage. In England and the United States, she still appeared on more platforms than she cared to count, and she was always greeted by such loud bursts of applause that she would playfully clap her own hands over her ears. Now Elizabeth Cady Stanton was the grand old lady of the woman's rights movement, just as Lucretia Mott had been in her own younger days.

Even though the cause of equality had not advanced either as far or as fast as Mrs. Stanton would have liked, much progress was finally being made. In state after state, various legal barriers preventing women from owning property or managing the money they earned were gradually being removed. Now a number of fine colleges accepted women students. It was no longer unheard of for a girl to study law or medicine, and many other kinds of employment were opening to female applicants.

On the matter of securing equal pay for equal work, the record was much less encouraging. And marriage and divorce laws still discriminated unfairly against women. However, Mrs. Stanton's main source of disappointment had to do with the most important item on her program back in Seneca Falls.

Women still could not vote for the President of the United States. But even so, the events of recent years gave her grounds for not losing hope. In the Wyoming Territory, the men of the West had proved their openmindedness by granting their wives and sisters all of the same political rights they themselves enjoyed. Dozens of communities all over the country were giving women the right to vote in local elections, and there already were many women serving on school boards or park committees. At the same time, Susan Anthony's constant efforts in the nation's capital had begun bearing results.

During the late 1880's, the Republican party's platform included what Mrs. Stanton laughingly called "a splinter"—a single sentence stating that woman suffrage should, at the least, be seriously considered. More to the point, pro-suffrage sentiment kept increasing in Congress. Now a suffrage amendment was being introduced at the beginning of every new session, and a Senate committee had already held hearings to consider the proposal on several occasions.

Each time, Mrs. Stanton appeared as the National Woman Suffrage Association's main speaker. In 1890 a new hearing was scheduled, and Miss Anthony once more begged her friend to come down to Washington. At the age of seventy-five, Mrs. Stanton shook her head. It did no good to keep sending "the same old war horse" to address the senators, she protested. Surely one of the many bright young women who had recently enlisted in the cause could make a better impression on these gentlemen.

But she was overruled. A number of the lawmakers informally let Miss Anthony know it was Mrs. Stanton they wished to hear, and so once again she boarded a train for Washington. This time her trip was not quite

Mrs. Stanton testifying before a Senate committee in Washington
Collections of The New York Public Library,
Astor, Lenox and Tilden Foundations

in vain. For the first time in American history, a report favoring a constitutional amendment giving women the right to vote was adopted by a committee of the United States Senate.

Not that the entire lawmaking body was now bound to approve the new amendment. It did not do so. The Senate as a whole was not yet ready, in 1890, to take this step. Nevertheless, no one with any interest in woman suffrage could deny that a major milestone had just been passed. Now it was only a matter of time till the amendment was adopted.

Even Lucy Stone had to agree. By now she was old and ill, but she generously gave full credit for this exciting new development to Susan Anthony and Lizzie Stanton, whose judgment she had disputed twenty years before. She had thought they were wrong to press for federal action, and that the only sensible course was to work toward suffrage in each separate state.

But in 1890, Lucy Stone also had her own reason to rejoice. Her policy scored a victory, too. In that same year, the Wyoming Territory was admitted to the Union as the forty-fourth state. Yet in one respect, it was the first. Now for the first time anywhere under the Stars and Stripes, in the new state of Wyoming women had full political equality with men.

So both wings of the suffrage movement had cause for celebrating, and the lapse of time had long since softened the bitterness that had made them break apart back in 1869. Thus with happy tears in their eyes, the three elderly women became friends again in 1890, and when the American Woman Suffrage Association and the National Woman Suffrage Association merged, they all pledged their allegiance to the newly formed National American Woman Suffrage Association. While Lucy Stone and Susan Anthony and Lizzie Stanton hugged each other on the platform of a Washington meeting hall, women throughout the audience cheered and waved their handkerchiefs.

The sensitive issue of choosing the combined group's president was solved more easily than anyone could have expected. Because of her illness, Lucy Stone said she must retire from active service. By a unanimous vote, the convention then selected Elizabeth Cady Stanton to lead it.

Mrs. Stanton thought she still felt as healthy as ever. However, her appetite for apple pie had not decreased. She was only of somewhat less than middle height, but now she weighed nearly 180 pounds. After being obliged to climb even a short flight of steps, she had to rest several minutes till she could catch her breath.

Moreover, she had lost her taste for constantly being on the go. So she served only two years as the president of the reunited association before positively insisting that Susan Anthony take over for her.

Susan's face had grown sharper, not rounder, with the passage of the years. To pose for a camera was a trying experience, she thought, and as a result photographs of her almost always pictured a sour-looking old spinster. Yet those who knew her warmth at first hand not only admired but loved her, and her elevation to the top post in the woman's movement won wide approval.

Still, the virtual retirement of Mrs. Stanton left a gap no one else could fill. Good old Lizzie! Nobody could make a hen convention laugh and cheer the way she could. In 1895, on her eightieth birthday, her friends tried to tell her how they felt about her. They hired the Metropolitan Opera House in New York City, and instead of any musical program they presented a whole evening of tributes to Lizzie Stanton.

While she sat up on the stage in her best black velvet,

Mrs. Stanton on her eightieth birthday

Elizabeth Cady Stanton Papers,
Vassar College Library

surrounded by all of her closest friends who were still alive, speaker after speaker searched for words with which to honor her. When she finally rose and replied to all this praise, she could not resist shaking her head with mock sadness.

It was an odd experience, she said, to attend your own funeral.

But Mrs. Stanton had no intention of departing from the scene quite yet. Although her travels now had to be limited, she still enjoyed the busy schedule she set herself in the New York apartment she shared with her widowed daughter, Maggie. Mornings, she wrote letters or articles for magazines, or else worked on the quirky book she was compiling about her own religious ideas. After lunch and a nap, she received a constant stream of callers. She read every sort of literature till her eyesight began failing, and then she hired students from nearby Columbia University to read to her. She even managed to bake some of her own favorite cakes after she could no longer walk without leaning on a cane. Maggie, or one of the students, would set out all the ingredients on a table, then Mrs. Stanton would sit there doing the mixing according to her own method.

She rejoiced that she had lived to see the turn of the century, and even when her eyes became so weak that she could hardly see a piece of paper on her work table she still dashed off letters every day. Her last letter, it happened, was written to President Theodore Roosevelt. She told him he would be sure to go down in history if he supported the woman suffrage amendment.

Then, on October 26, 1902, at the ripe age of eighty-seven, Elizabeth Cady Stanton died in her sleep.

Not quite eighteen years later, the nineteenth amendment to the Constitution took effect. It said:

> The right of citizens of the United States to vote shall not be denied or abridged by the United States or by any state on account of sex.
>
> Congress shall have power to enforce this article by appropriate legislation.

At last, in 1920, Lizzie Stanton's own place in American history was secure.

Would she have been disappointed if she had known that in the 1970's the women of the United States would still be fighting for full equality? Or would she have been right up there on the platform, applauding as a new generation made new demands for woman's liberation? Her own words give the answer.

"Lifting woman into her proper place is the mightiest revolution the world has yet known," Mrs. Stanton said. "It may be that more than half a century is needed to accomplish this."

SUGGESTIONS FOR FURTHER READING

Beatty, Patricia, *Hail Columbia*. New York: William Morrow & Co., Inc., 1970.

Bolton, Sarah K., *Lives of Girls Who Became Famous*. New York: Thomas Y. Crowell Co., rev. ed., 1949.

Commager, Henry Steele, *Crusaders for Freedom*. New York: Doubleday & Co., Inc., 1962.

Coolidge, Olivia, *Women's Rights: The Suffrage Movement in America 1848–1920*. New York: E. P. Dutton & Co., Inc., 1966.

Faber, Doris, *I Will Be Heard: The Life of William Lloyd Garrison*. New York: Lothrop, Lee & Shepard Co., 1970.

———, *Petticoat Politics: How American Women Won the Right to Vote*. New York: Lothrop, Lee & Shepard Co., 1967.

Severn, Bill, *Free but Not Equal: How Women Won the Right to Vote*. New York: Julian Messner, Inc., 1967.

NOTE: The books listed are suggested for young readers who may be interested in finding out more about the woman's rights movement, but it should be noted that *Oh, Lizzie!* is based largely on the writings of Mrs. Stanton and her contemporaries, and this material is not readily available. For their help in locating old letters and memoirs, I would like to thank all those who assisted me on the staffs of the New York Public Library, the New York Society Library, the Westchester County Library System, and the Vassar College Library where the bulk of Mrs. Stanton's personal papers were deposited by her daughters.

D.F.

INDEX